THE PROFESSIONAL MANAGER

the professional manager

DOUGLAS McGREGOR

Late Sloan Professor of Management
Massachusetts Institute of Technology

EDITED BY CAROLINE McGREGOR

Alfred P. Sloan School of Management
Massachusetts Institute of Technology

AND WARREN G. BENNIS

Provost,
State University of New York at Buffalo

HD
31
.M22

McGRAW-HILL BOOK COMPANY   NEW YORK • ST. LOUIS • SAN FRANCISCO

TORONTO • LONDON • SYDNEY

EDITORS' PREFACE

We wish it were possible to present the reader with a finished book exactly as Douglas McGregor would have done it. This has been our preoccupation, even if we have not measured up to it. Actually, Doug wrote most of the present manuscript during the summer of 1964, shortly before his untimely death in October of the same year.

The history of this manuscript seems typical of the way he approached any task. He set up some propositions, talked them, tested them in public presentations and in practice, revised, and took some satisfaction in the distilled product although this too was subject to further change. This might explain the fact that he was content to put the manuscript away without regrets after the summer and look forward to another seasoning period provided by teaching and other work. It is in this sense of seasoning and further growth that he saw the work as unfinished.

In thinking about this style of operating, the experience he had in writing a paper on measurement with the help of Professor E. G. Boring (the "Chief") in graduate school may be recalled. Boring had expressed the view that the paper should be published, and he said he would be glad to help Doug work it into shape. Many versions were patiently edited by Boring with copious notes until one came back with the single comment: "The curve is asymptotic to zero." The original plan was a joint publication, and it ended up with a footnote by Boring, which Doug prized. Doug often said that this experience was one of his high points in learning, and he continued to use the technique of rewriting and rethinking his material.

He extended the process considerably to include more resources from the environment, the feedback from presenting ideas, and the successes and failures in actual practice. He committed himself to writing with great care and a real desire to share any understanding he had acquired, but with some sense of skepticism that the written word would produce significant change.

Doug saw himself as an educator rather than a writer. Writing was part of it and one of his pleasures, a tool for most of his work in teaching and consulting. His famous *Human Side* probably did more to educate managers—mainly because it spoke with a rare empathy to the professional manager—than any other book written in this decade.

Four themes recur throughout this volume with such intensity that there is no mistaking their salience for Doug. The first theme is expressed in Chapter 1, where he discusses the importance of *theory*—assumptions about life may be a more apt phrase—and how it influences our worldview. His entire discussion of cosmology and perception, which grew out of his lifelong concern with "prediction of social events,"[1] stems from the pivotal role he assigns to cosmology.

The second theme, underlying the entire volume but most forcibly presented in Chapter 1, is connected with his concern for theory. Doug thought that practitioners, particularly industrial managers, are extremely vulnerable to emotional (sometimes unconscious) reactions which are never adequately reckoned with and which interfere with their perception of reality. He saw the culture of management as inhospitable to the expression of natural human responses and that this taboo led to a dissonant underground world where feelings were guiltily bootlegged in, or worse, where they unwittingly entered into and subverted important decisions. Thus, Doug emphasizes rational-emotive man. Man is a rational being, he argues, but the only way he can realize his grandeur is to recognize and come to terms with his emotional and human side.

In *The Human Side*, Doug contributed heavily to the idea of "integration," a creative invention of how the individual and the organization come to terms with each other. In this volume, he places the idea of integration within the framework of a *transactional* concept of power and influence. This third theme, which allows him to advance much farther than he could before, develops the idea that influence can be transactional (a high degree of mutuality) and need not be a "win-lose" affair, in which if A gets 100 units, B gets zero and if A gets 90 units, B gets 10, etc. He takes pains to show that when certain social elements are present (such as trust and mutual support), there is no need for concern about "power equalization" or the loss of responsibility and status.

---

[1] It is interesting to note that some of his first research (in the late thirties) was on the prediction of social events. For a retrospective sampling of his written work, see *Leadership and Motivation: The Essays of Douglas McGregor.* Cambridge, Mass.: The M.I.T. Press, 1966.

Finally, Doug was becoming more interested in the problem of managing differences and the ways in which management could cope with the necessity of diversity and incongruities as well as the potentialities for collaboration and teamwork. His final chapter was a first approximation of dealing with this dilemma.

There are other themes that the reader will undoubtedly pick up, for we speak with no special wisdom or omniscience about his work except for close colleagueship and love, neither of which guarantee critical judgment. What we tried to do in tackling this assignment was to keep the goal of rendering this book to as many of Doug's readers as we could in the shortest possible time. We did add a sentence or two here and there and made minor changes when we thought it would clarify or improve the text. In some cases, we added a summary at the end of a chapter or a reference for the reader who wished to follow up with more reading.

Many people have helped in the presentation of this volume. Edgar H. Schein, Richard Beckhard, and Mason Haire have shared with us some of the important decisions and early work regarding the publication of the manuscript; Ed Schein was particularly helpful in making valuable suggestions for organizing the material. Rensis Likert and Charles A. Myers also read the manuscript and added their help, both editorial and substantive, as well as encouragement for the task. To Douglass V. Brown and Howard W. Johnson we owe a real debt for their wisdom and support at all times. Another member of the team is Patti Macpherson, Doug's former secretary, who gave valuable help in locating material and generous assistance with typing.

The first two chapters were published as an essay entitled "The Manager, Human Nature and Human Sciences" in *Leadership and Motivation: Essays by Douglas McGregor,* edited by Warren G. Bennis and Edgar H. Schein, a memorial volume published by the M.I.T. Press, Cambridge, Massachusetts, in 1966. It is reprinted here with some changes with the formal consent of the M.I.T. Press.

Two of Doug's close friends helped us to complete Chapter 7. Kilburn LeCompte edited and brought up to date the section describing the program he directed at The Bell Telephone Company of Pennsylvania. John Paul Jones added statements of policies and objectives worked out in the Organization Department at Union Carbide Corporation. It seems especially appropriate that these two case studies are included in a chapter on organization of managerial work since Doug so enjoyed his association with both companies.

In locating and confirming references, we are indebted to Rensis Likert, Eric L. Trist, Robert R. Blake, Lawrence K. Williams, John G. Hooven, and George H. Murray, Jr.

There are many others whose friendship and influence Doug valued, who may rightly feel that they have a part in the ideas and aims expressed in this book. At the risk of serious omissions, we shall mention only a few: Edwin G. Boring, Gordon Allport, Irving Knickerbocker, Leland P. Bradford, and Jay W. Forrester.

One last word. Doug had not settled on a title for this book as far as we know. The felicitous title of his *Human Side* is unmatchable. Already, it bespeaks a way of life, a philosophy. We decided on *The Professional Manager* because it reflects Doug's concern and commitment toward developing the profession of management through bridging its goals with the aims, values, and methodology of behavioral science. We hope this book can accelerate more communication and commitment toward this end.

WARREN G. BENNIS

CAROLINE McGREGOR

CONTENTS

INTRODUCTION

In 1960 Douglas McGregor published *The Human Side of Enterprise*. In this book he gave to the academic and industrial community a set of values about people in organizations which were widely held but had not been clearly stated or examined. Ironically, Doug did not intend to state values. Instead, he intended to point out that the assumptions upon which traditional principles of management rested were out of step with what psychology has learned about human behavior. He meant his book to be a plea for self-examination on the part of managers, in the hope that they would examine their own assumptions and bring them into line with what is known and what they wished to accomplish.

However, I have encountered few readers, particularly among managers, who took this to be Doug's primary message. Instead, Doug's book has been seen as a plea for an attitude, a set of values toward people, symbolized by the term *Theory Y*. The essence of this attitude is to trust people, to grant them the power to motivate and control themselves, to believe in their capacity to integrate their own personal values with the goals of the organization. Doug believed that individual needs can and should be integrated with organizational goals. In the extreme, Theory Y has meant democratic processes in management, giving people a greater voice in the making of decisions and trusting them to contribute rationally and loyally without surrounding them with elaborate control structures.

In my own contacts with Doug, I often found him to be discouraged by the degree to which Theory Y had become as monolithic a set of principles as those of Theory X, the overgeneralizations which Doug was fighting. He wanted Theory Y to be a *realistic* view, in which one examined one's assumptions, tested them against reality, and then chose a managerial strategy that made sense in terms of one's diagnosis of reality. Yet few readers were willing to acknowledge that the content of Doug's book made such a neutral point, or that Doug's own presentation of his point of view was that coldly scientific. Because Doug himself believed in people, he communicated his values both in his personal presence and in his writing. But he was bothered by this fact. Not that he did not cherish his own values; but he had a message for management theory that went beyond them and that he had not yet found a way to communicate.

The essence of the message is that people react not to an objective world, but to a world fashioned out of their own perceptions, assumptions, and theories of what the world is like. Managers, like all the rest of us, can be trapped by these assumptions into inappropriate and ineffective decisions. McGregor wished passionately to release all of us from this trap, by getting us to be aware of how each of our worlds is of our own making. Once we become aware we can choose—and it was the process of free choice that we believe was Doug's ultimate value.

A second strong force was acting on Doug. He found many colleagues and students who said, "We agree with your Theory Y vision of man, but we don't know how to put it into practice. Tell us how to think or feel or behave differently as managers." *The present volume grew out of the twin needs to reexplain his own epistemological position and provide a more concrete description of the implications of various sets of assumptions about man.*

This book shows Doug's struggles to provide people with alternatives so that they could choose more freely, and it reflects his own growing vision of how one might manage human effort in industrial organizations if one did have more faith in the human capacity to work productively and creatively.

Doug was responding in his various chapters to the plea all of us have heard all too often: Your theories are fine but they won't work; show us what to do differently so that we can see for ourselves; show us how to apply the theories. Ultimately Doug's answer would, of course, have had to be that each person must find his own answers to these questions. But he did have a growing conviction that certain key issues which managers dealt with daily could be illuminated in a helpful manner and could provide more bases for choice. So he set out to discuss in greater detail than he ever had in previous writings his view of how the manager can think about and deal with himself—his own role and style, his own power, the issue of control over others, the organization of work, the problem of teamwork, and, perhaps most importantly, the problem of how to manage conflict creatively.

The reader will find this material more concrete, more detailed, and more oriented toward the immediate day-to-day problems of the manager. Yet, running through it is the basic theory which Doug tried to communicate. He did not succeed in obtaining the closure he himself was looking for, and perhaps the most important lesson in his own experience is that such closure is premature. We do not yet know enough about human behavior or organizations to lay down a set of principles which can be proclaimed to be the answer to the problems of our managerial society. Doug can remind us of this fact through his own struggles and efforts. In this final work he has provided some guidelines which may help each of us to come to terms with our own assumptions and thereby liberate us to see the world more accurately and wisely.

Edgar H. Schein

INTRODUCTION

Since the halfway point of the twentieth century, we have seen an explosion of knowledge and technology that has changed life for all of us. Increasingly significant to men entrusted with the stewardship of organizations is the rapid growth of knowledge in the social sciences, particularly those concerned with man's behavior in his organizational environment. Emerging as a central concern in the sixties is the utilization of this knowledge, the application of behavioral science research to the practice of management and the direction of organizations.

Doug McGregor was in the vanguard of this movement. He had a real mission to create a bridge between the producers of knowledge and the users of knowledge. He was fond of quoting the expression of his colleague, Kurt Lewin: "Nothing is so practical as a good theory." At the same time he always had the realities of organizational life in mind when he was developing theory.

I can illustrate the ways in which McGregor used his influence to bring together the members of the academic and industrial communities from my own relationship with him. When I started in the management consulting field, in the early fifties, he helped me learn to use the knowledge from the behavioral sciences as a way of working with clients. Some years later, as a part of his continuing effort to integrate theory and practice, he asked me to join his faculty group at the Alfred P. Sloan School of Management at the Massachusetts Institute of Technology.

McGregor had real "membership" in many worlds. He was considered "one of us" by his colleagues in academic life, by the members of the consulting fraternity, and by managers of organizations throughout the world. (His writings are the most dramatic example of his "multiple memberships.") The strong identification he created in everyone who met him personally or through his writings was, in my opinion, a considerable factor in the tremendous impact of his book *The Human Side of Enterprise.*

In that book, he was examining the assumptions behind various managerial strategies and defining some implications for various management processes. He was producing new and enlarged theory about *knowledge-based* assumptions. It was a source of some disappointment to him that some managers reacted to it as a "how to" book of managerial strategy; some others saw it as primarily a statement of humanistic values. He himself hoped it would be read and used as a basis for sharpened self-examination, better diagnosis, and more sophisticated choice points in determining managerial strategy.

In this final effort, he is pushing his inquiry further into man's view of his world. As with "assumptions" in the earlier work, here he tests the concept of man's "cosmology" against the issues of organizational behavior and management.

The scientist McGregor presents a hypothesis of a relationship between the nature of man and his view of his world. He examines this relationship as it applies to a series of dilemmas: role and role conflict, relationship of personal style and managerial strategy, and the appropriate use of managerial power.

The utilizer McGregor looks at each of these dilemmas in actual organizational settings with practical examples to test his hypotheses.

This book offers no panaceas or cookbook solutions, but rather a way of approaching the life of business and the business of life, which pretty well defines the way Doug McGregor lived.

Richard Beckhard

THE PROFESSIONAL MANAGER

part one

THE MANAGER
AND THE HUMAN
SCIENCES

the manager's view of reality: cosmology

INTRODUCTION

The manager's view of reality is of course far wider and more complex than the following discussion will suggest. It includes his view of the physical world and, at a deeper level, his beliefs, however implicit, concerning "the meaning of it all."

The function of cosmology[1] is to bring some semblance of order to experiences which otherwise would be so confusing that there would be no basis for action. It is difficult to imagine the anxiety that would result if man had no conception of cause and effect, no way of ordering his perception of reality and his experience with it. Thus, a cosmology is importantly associated with the individual's basic security, his confidence that he can cope successfully with physical and social reality.

The individual never experiences a complete lack of order in reality (except perhaps in early childhood), because he is endowed with a nervous system that enables him to perceive and remember selectively, to generalize, to relate, to discriminate, and to organize with respect to situations and events. Inevitably, he develops strong needs to find subjective order in what objectively is massive complexity. In fact, his needs frequently lead him to impose order on reality even when it is not objectively there. His possession of these characteristics, plus the fact that he lives in a culture in which there are already existing ordered views of reality, provides him with the basis for developing a cosmology.

In some sense every individual's cosmology is unique. In other respects all individuals share common beliefs about reality. However, no cosmology *is* reality; it is a human perception of reality. It is like a map of a territory that has been only partly explored and perhaps never will be completely known. The traveler therefore must rely to some extent on his own wits, using his map but remembering always that it is an imperfect representation of reality.

I try in this chapter to indicate a few ways in which the growth of behavioral science knowledge has changed the map upon which the managerial traveler in our society has tended to rely. But my analogy appears to break down, because some of this knowledge contradicts the evidence provided by the manager's own experience. He finds that the map does not correspond to his direct observa-

---

[1] *"Cosmology" is defined as the theory of the universe as a whole and the laws governing it. (Eds.)*

tion of the territory through which he is traveling. This is not, however, an unusual circumstance, nor is the tendency to reject the map that contradicts experience.

All of us have come to terms in some fashion with findings in *physical* science that contradict our direct experience. Such knowledge asserts that the sun and the planets do not rise and set as they appear to do, that ordinary physical objects are in fact not solid as they seem to be, that invisible and unexperienced biological organisms affect our health and well-being, that what appear to be simple cause-effect relationships are in fact extremely complex.

Similarly, behavioral science knowledge involves assertions about the nature of man and of cause and effect in human behavior that challenge direct experience. Some of these findings are backed by sufficient research to give one considerable confidence that they are true. Some are still subject to controversy; like all scientific knowledge, they represent partial truth, and there may be material changes as new knowledge accumulates. Let us now consider some of this knowledge and determine its effect on the manager's view of cosmology.

APPLYING BEHAVIORAL SCIENCE KNOWLEDGE TO MANAGEMENT

Useful scientific knowledge consists in (1) identification of the factors, characteristics, or variables that are sufficient and necessary causes of a given set of phenomena; and (2) statements about the relationships among these factors that are associated with changes in the phenomena. Thus the performance P of an individual at work in an industrial organization is a function of certain characteristics of the individual I, including his knowledge, skills, motivation, attitudes, and certain aspects of the environmental situation E, including the nature of his job, the rewards associated with his performance, and the leadership provided him.

$$P = f(I_{a,b,c,d} \ldots E_{m,n,o,p} \ldots)$$

The relationships among these variables are many and complex. Existing behavioral science knowledge does not permit precise quantitative statements of most of them, but much that is useful can be said about their form and nature.

Perhaps the most general statement of the potential contribution that behavioral science can make to management would be this: Our present knowledge indicates that there are a number of important characteristics of individuals *and* of the work environment which conventional management practice does not take into account. The variables that most managers do recognize are necessary, but they are not sufficient to explain organized human effort. Behavioral science affords the possibility of improving organized human effort by identifying additional variables and their interrelationships so that, once recognized, they may be taken into account in managerial practice.

It is obvious, and demonstrably true scientifically, that man's behavior is influenced by certain characteristics of his environment. When we speak of motivating people, we are referring to the possibility of creating relationships between characteristics of man and characteristics of his environment that will result in certain desired behavior. "Reward" and "punishment" are the terms in common use to describe generally the environmental characteristics that are controlled to influence behavior.

It is important to recognize, however, that what is involved is always a *relationship* between E variables and I variables. Giving or withholding a particular sum of money or a particular kind of food will affect a particular individual's behavior in certain ways, *depending on his characteristics*. The offer of beef to a Hindu and a Christian will affect their behavior quite differently. A glass of water may have a powerful influence on a man dying of thirst and none on a man who already has access to water. A ten-dollar monthly raise in pay will affect a clerk and a top executive differently.

The relationships are indeed complex. They involve the individual's capabilities, his goals, his needs, his expectations, his attitudes, his perceptions concerning the scarcity of the reward that is being given or withheld. They involve relationships not only of reward or punishment to the individual, but of other characteristics of the environment. The threat of discharge will affect the behavior of an accounting clerk and a nuclear physicist differently in United States industry under present economic conditions. Knowledge about cause and effect in human behavior rests on knowledge of the relevant characteristics of I and E (which ones are "necessary" and which are "sufficient" to account for the behavior) and on knowledge about the relationships that hold between these characteristics.

There is a substantial amount of unified knowledge about some of these relationships today; some are less well known and often disputed; and virtually nothing is known about others. A detailed analysis of the current state of knowledge would have little value for the manager. I propose, therefore, to present only certain general findings that seem to me to be fairly well established and, in addition, to be particularly relevant to the concerns of industrial managers. Even so, I shall ignore many qualifications and complications.

REWARDS AND PUNISHMENTS AS INCENTIVES

One important body of knowledge has to do with two quite different kinds of motivational relationships. The first, and by far the most recognized and utilized today, involves what are called *extrinsic* rewards and punishments—they exist as characteristics of the environment, and their relationship to behavior is relatively direct. Money is the most obvious of them, but fringe benefits, promotion, praise, recognition, criticism, and social acceptance and rejection are other examples.

Intrinsic rewards, on the other hand, are inherent in the activity itself: The reward is the achievement of the goal. Intrinsic rewards cannot be *directly* controlled externally, although characteristics of the environment can enhance or limit the individual's opportunities to obtain them. Thus, achievements of knowledge or skill, of autonomy, of self-respect, of solutions to problems, are examples. So are some of the rewards associated with genuine altruism: giving love and help to others.

Management has rather fully exploited the possibilities of influencing behavior by controlling extrinsic rewards and punishments (although there are some important exceptions that will be considered later). In general, however, far less attention has been paid to intrinsic rewards. There are, I believe, two major reasons. The first is the difficulty in establishing a direct link between these rewards and performance. One can give money as a promotion for superior performance. The causal linkage is obvious to the recipient, as is the source of the reward. But one cannot give the sense of accomplishment that accompanies the individual's or group's recognition of having found a solution to a difficult and important problem. (This is quite different from the *extrinsic* reward of praise for the achievement.) In short, management cannot so easily or directly control intrinsic rewards. The individual *can* be prevented from obtaining such rewards—for example, by close supervision that gives him no opportunity to solve problems on his own. It is interesting and significant, however, that under such circumstances people will often obtain this reward by ingenious solutions that involve a kind of sabotage of management's control systems. "Beating the system" is a widely played game in which intrinsic rewards are highly motivational.

The second reason for management's failure to exploit the possibilities of intrinsic rewards is closely associated with beliefs about the nature of man that have been prominent in Western culture for at least two centuries. We need not become involved in the philosophical debate concerning the relationship between mind and body except to recognize that a central issue has been whether man's behavior can be explained in terms of purely mechanical analogies or whether it is necessary to assume the existence of "forces" that may be independent of physical law. However managers have resolved this issue personally, managerial practice appears to reflect at least a tacit belief that motivating people *to work* is a "mechanical" problem.

There are certain similarities between this view of man at work and Newton's laws of motion. To a considerable degree, man has been perceived to be like a physical body at rest. The application of external force is required to set him in motion—to motivate him to work. Consequently, extrinsic rewards and punishments are the obvious and appropriate forces to be utilized in controlling organized human effort.

Probably few managers today would accept these assertions as true of their own managerial philosophy. Most would insist that they recognize man to be to some degree self-activated. They would point particularly to that small proportion of the population that includes the "natural leaders." These men are ambitious by nature; they possess initiative and a desire to assume responsibility; they do not require the application of external force to set them in motion, although of course they are responsive to extrinsic rewards.

In addition, it would be argued that even the average man is self-activated in certain ways. He expends energy in play, in pursuing hobbies, and in other pleasure-seeking activities. Some individuals expend considerable energy, without obvious external cause, in destructive activities that undermine managerial objectives. They are self-motivated, but negatively.

The real point, it would then be argued, is not that man is set in motion only by external forces, but that the internal forces that activate him are—except for "the few"—antithetical to the requirements of organized human effort. He can be directed into productive effort at work only by means of extrinsic rewards and by punishments that counteract his "negative" motivation.

Whichever view one takes, then, the outcome in terms of managerial strategy is identical: Extrinsic rewards and punishments are the appropriate methods for controlling the behavior of the great majority of human beings.

This is an important issue. If human nature is essentially as thus described, intrinsic rewards and punishments have little or no value for the manager. In fact, a major part of the managerial task is to counteract natural human tendencies that are opposed to the goals of organization.

A view that is often expressed by managers today says that most people want maximum rewards for minimum effort. They want security—guarantees of employment and protection against most of the hazards of life. They tend to be indifferent or even negative toward reasonable standards of performance. As managers who hold this view see the situation, these characteristics of human nature are being steadily reinforced by government, labor unions, and some managements that have the unfortunate tendency to be too soft.

If, on the other hand, the self-activated characteristics of man are not *by their nature* antithetical to the requirements of organized human effort, the possibility exists that they could become assets to management rather than liabilities. If some substantial majority of human beings are not prevented *by nature* from being like the few (at least in a motivational sense), intrinsic rewards and punishments could be significant tools of management.

It is this view of human nature that is supported by much current knowledge and enlightened practice. The mechanical view is not wrong; it is insufficient to account for a considerable amount of man's behavior at work. A number of research studies have provided evidence of many ways in which intrinsic rewards can yield higher performance and reduce opposition to organization goals, and of many ways in which intrinsic punishment (often unwittingly imposed by management) can have the opposite consequences.

We shall examine some of these findings and their implications for managerial practice in later chapters. One example will serve as an illustration for the moment.

A series of studies in IBM revealed that the introduction of work standards in certain departments by a strategy utilizing extrinsic rewards and punishments brought about increased performance and also lowered morale. In certain other departments, managers opposed to this strategy brought about equivalent improvement *without* negative influences on morale. The essential difference in the latter case lay in the utilization of intrinsic rewards associated with the desire of workers to control their own fate, i.e., to have a greater degree of autonomy than was possible with the *imposition* of standards that was involved in the former case.[2]

These studies did not investigate the negative side effects, other than morale, that have been found typically to be associated with the conventional strategies of introducing work standards. In terms of cost and efficiency, these additional side effects (various methods invented by workers for beating the system) have been frequently demonstrated to be substantial.

A THEORY OF MOTIVATION

Strictly speaking, the answer to the question managers so often ask of behavioral scientists—How do you motivate people?—is: You don't. Man is by nature motivated. He is an *organic* system, not a mechanical one. Inputs of energy (sunlight, food, water, etc.) are transformed by him into outputs of behavior (including intellectual activities and emotional responses, as well as observable actions). His behavior is influenced by relationships between his charac-

[2] D. Sirota, "A Study of Work Measurement," *Sixteenth Annual Proceedings of the Industrial Relations Research Association,* 1964; D. Sirota and S. M. Klein, "Employees' Attitudes toward Aspects of Work Measurement," *Personnel Research Studies* (IBM), 1961.

teristics as an organic system I and the environment E. [Performance $P = f(\text{individual} \ldots \text{environment})$] Creating these relationships is a matter of *releasing* his energy in certain ways rather than others. We do not motivate him, because he *is* motivated. When he is not, he is dead. This is the sense in which the behavioral scientist distinguishes between an organic and a purely mechanical theory of human nature.

In an earlier volume,[3] I attempted to summarize a view of the motivational nature of man associated prominently with the name of Abraham Maslow.[4] This theory has gained considerable support from other behavioral scientists. Its central thesis is that human needs are organized in a hierarchy, with physical needs for survival at the base. At progressively higher levels are needs for security, social interaction, and ego satisfaction. Generally speaking, when lower-level needs are reasonably well satisfied, successively higher levels of needs become relatively more important as motivators of behavior.

The relationships are by no means as simple as this brief statement implies. For example, "reasonable satisfaction" is culturally defined. A subsistence level of satisfaction of physical needs in our society today is far higher than that, say, in the villages of India. Moreover, man's higher-level needs are not completely absent, even at bare subsistence levels. He seeks ways of achieving his social and ego needs, even when he is relatively deprived with respect to his lower needs. Even in circumstances of severe deprivation, many may rebel against social and political restrictions in the interests of their higher needs. However, less energy is available if most of it must be used for sheer survival. In general, the relative strength of human needs is consistent with the hierarchy described above. Another qualification is that severe deprivation of lower-level needs in early life may warp the individual's adjustment in a variety of ways and accentuate their importance for him permanently (except as psychotherapy may later modify his adjustment). Thus we find people with fixations on money, for example, or security, or power.

Man's goals associated with his physical, security, and social needs are achieved largely by means of extrinsic rewards that are

[3] D. McGregor, *The Human Side of Enterprise.* New York: McGraw-Hill Book Company, 1960.
[4] A. H. Maslow, *Motivation and Personality.* New York: Harper & Row, Publishers, Incorporated, 1954.

controlled by others. It is because of this that mutual trust is such a basic requirement of effective organizational relationships. In its absence there is no assurance to employees of equity in the administration of wages and salaries, promotion, or discipline. In its absence also, management must establish tight controls and exercise close surveillance over employees.

Some of the goals associated with ego needs are achieved by means of extrinsic rewards—for example, recognition and status. Others, as noted earlier, are achieved solely by intrinsic rewards. The difficulty with intrinsic rewards, from management's point of view, is in utilizing them for purposes of control. I have argued above that part of the problem lies in the mistaken assumption that these needs are by their nature antithetical to the purposes of the industrial organization—that they are expressed in pleasure-seeking activities and not through work. Let us examine this assumption further.

If the expenditure of energy is work, it is clear that human beings often work hard at their hobbies and in other pleasureful activities. They work hard in acquiring skills or knowledge *that they wish to acquire.* They work hard in the service of causes to which they are committed—in civic or political or religious or social or humanitarian organizations. They expend energy in organized artistic activities—music or theater or graphic arts.

It is often argued that most people are by nature dependent—that they prefer not to accept responsibility but to be led. If we observe their behavior on the job, the generalization appears to hold rather widely. Yet it is surprising how many of the same people not only accept but seek responsibility in a variety of organized activities away from the job.

Intrinsic rewards are significant in all these activities, although extrinsic rewards of status, recognition, and social acceptance are involved as well. The basic point is that intrinsic rewards are not associated exclusively with human activities of the kind that are defined as recreational. Nor are such activities carried on exclusively outside of organizational settings. It is not human nature that excludes the pursuit of goals yielding intrinsic rewards from the job environment. It is not human nature that defines pleasure-seeking activities as nonproductive. Human needs can be satisfied in a great variety of environments. With the exception of a very few (such as sleep and sex), they can be satisfied through activities that management would define as productive, as well as through activities that management would define otherwise.

It is my belief that a realistic perception of man in these respects has been obscured in our culture for a very long time by the moral conviction that pleasure is sinful and must therefore be disassociated from productive work. To earn his daily bread by the sweat of his brow is the punishment meted out to man ever since Adam and Eve were driven from the Garden; it is through painful and unpleasant effort that man atones for his sins and develops strength of character; what is good cannot be obtained through pleasureful activity. Certainly this is not the full explanation, but the influence of this social norm in our society is strong and pervasive.

The motivational theory under discussion asserts that man—if he is freed to some extent from using most of his energy to obtain the necessities of life and a degree of security from the major vicissitudes—will by nature begin to pursue goals associated with his higher-level needs. These include needs for a degree of control over his own fate, for self-respect, for using and increasing his talents, for responsibility, for achievement both in the sense of status and recognition and in the sense of personal development and effective problem solving. Thus freed, he will also seek in many ways to satisfy more fully his physical needs for recreation, relaxation, and play. Management has been well aware of the latter tendency; it has not often recognized the former, or at least it has not taken into account its implications for managerial strategy.

IMPLICATIONS OF THE THEORY FOR MANAGEMENT

A statement of strategy that has long seemed to me to be consistent with the goals of economic enterprise on the one hand, and with behavioral science knowledge of the motivational nature of man on the other, is this: Management must seek to create conditions (an organizational environment) such that members of the organization at all levels can best achieve their own goals by directing their efforts toward the goals of the organization. With respect to lower-level needs, this places before management the task of providing extrinsic rewards, *on an equitable basis,* for all kinds of contributions to the success of the enterprise. Since management controls these rewards, and can therefore both give and withhold them, this task also involves the equitable administration of extrinsic punishments for negative contributions. Note that this statement is careful not to relate these rewards and punishments to compliance or noncompliance with *management's wishes*. It cannot be assumed—in fact, it is often untrue—that a given manager's wishes are the expression of the goals of the enterprise (even sometimes when he is a top-level executive).

With respect to higher-level ego needs (and some middle-level social needs) management's task is to provide opportunities for members of the organization to obtain intrinsic rewards from contributions to the success of the enterprise. Since management does not directly control such rewards, the problem of equity in their administration does not arise. The task is to provide an appropriate environment—one that will permit and encourage employees to seek intrinsic rewards *at work*. Its performance will involve managers at every level in an examination of the way work is organized; the nature and administration of managerial controls; the way responsibilities are assigned and supervised; the way goals are set, policies established, planning done—in short, almost every aspect of managerial practice.

Often the provision of opportunities for intrinsic rewards becomes a matter of removing restraints. Progress is rarely fast because people who have become accustomed to control through extrinsic rewards exclusively must learn new attitudes and habits before they can feel secure in accepting opportunities for intrinsic rewards at work. If there is not a fair degree of mutual trust, and some positive support, the whole idea may appear highly risky to them.

It will not be fruitful for management to undertake this task unless there is genuine open-mindedness (if not acceptance) with respect to the motivational character of human nature outlined in the preceding pages.[5]

[5] *In one area of industrial organizations—namely, the scientific research laboratory involved primarily in basic research—management has gone a considerable way toward accomplishing this task. The reasons for doing so have been largely connected with the problem of obtaining and keeping competent scientists, rather than with the acceptance of new ideas about human nature. (In fact, I have heard many managers assert vehemently that scientists are not at all representative of Homo sapiens!) I doubt that these results would have been achieved except for the external pressures that have almost literally forced changes in policy and practice on some of these managements. Those pressures are not evident to anything like the same degree in the rest of the industrial organization today. (Eds.)*

One of the generalizations which emerges from these considerations about motivation and human nature is this: When a manager asserts, on the basis of his experience and observation, that most people are by nature either indifferent or antagonistic toward the goals of the industrial enterprise, there is more than a small possibility that he may be confusing cause and effect. The indifference and hostility are often observable, but they may be the *result* of a managerial strategy that has, over a long period, provided adequate extrinsic rewards for lower-level needs but has ignored or even prevented the achievement of intrinsic rewards associated with higher-level needs. The former needs, being reasonably well satisfied, have become less motivational; the latter, being frustrated, are finding expression outside the organization (and perhaps also in the exercise of ingenuity to beat the system inside the organization).

Another generalization emerging from an organic conception of human nature is that all human relationships are *transactional*. Since the normal individual is not passive toward his environment, but is actively coping with it, *influence in any form is a two-way process.*

Raymond Bauer, in a penetrating analysis of research on social communication, indicates how behavioral scientists have gradually come to recognize that even communication by means of mass media ("obviously" a one-way form of influence) is transactional in significant ways. The reciprocal influence in social communication is not necessarily balanced—there may be inequities either way. The essential point is that it is never fully one way.[6]

The reactions of the influenced may not be directly or immediately observable to the influencer, but this does not mean they are absent.

The manager whose conception of cause and effect in human behavior is mechanical must rely on the "orneriness" of human nature for an explanation of the many forms of indifference or resistance to managerial influence. The only way he can conceive of to counteract them is to increase the threat of extrinsic punishment (which often aggravates the symptoms he is trying to eliminate).

The manager whose conception of cause and effect is organic will recognize the transactional character of influence. When he en-

[6] R. Bauer, "The Obstinate Audience: The Influence Process from the Point of View of Social Communications," *American Psychologist*, vol. 19, no. 5, pp. 319–328, May, 1964.

counters indifference or resistance, he will attribute the reaction
not to human nature, but to aspects of the relationship between E
variables and I variables that can be analyzed and probably corrected by *mutual* interaction.

The values in *participation* as a tactic of management do not lie
merely, or even primarily, in the fact that people like to be consulted about decisions affecting them. The significant point is that
participation, when it is sincere and genuine, is an open recognition
of the interactional character of influence. When resistance to or
sabotage of managerial decisions is anticipated, participation provides a natural method for minimizing or eliminating either in
advance.

Thus a manager's view of human nature powerfully influences
his selection of a strategy. (See Chapter 5 for a discussion of
managerial strategies.) His strategy, in turn, powerfully influences
the behavior of his subordinates. Naturally, he takes the evidence
provided by their behavior as proof of his views of human nature.
Such circular reactions can occur with incorrect or inadequate
beliefs about human nature as well as with adequate ones. Once
they are established, contrary evidence is often rejected on the
ground that it is inconsistent with directly observable reality.

Such situations are by no means limited to management or to
the behavioral sciences. They have been repeated countless times
throughout history in the physical sciences, as man has rejected
evidence contradicting his direct experience of reality. It is often
decades, and sometimes centuries, before these issues are finally
resolved.

PERCEIVED VERSUS OBJECTIVE REALITY

Another important property of human nature has been elaborated
as a result of behavioral science research. It is that human behavior
is seldom a *direct* response to objective reality, but is rather a
response to the individual's perception of that reality. A simple
reflex, such as the removal of the finger from a hot stove, appears
to be a direct response to reality. But even it is mediated by the
nervous system. Impulses must flow in through sensory nerves and
back out through nerves controlling muscular action before the
response can occur. Moreover, as a result of learning, the individual

may on occasion refrain from touching a stove in the belief that it is hot when in fact it is not. He responds to *his perception* of reality.

Human response to more complex aspects of reality involves higher levels of the nervous system that have certain important characteristics. Among the most important of these are the processes of selective perception and memory by which the individual organizes his perception of reality.

We recognize these processes readily enough in some circumstances. A common expression is: "That's not the way I see it." However, we tend to think of this phenomenon as being restricted to ambiguous situations such as those associated with politics or broad social issues. It is not easy to accept the fact that even our perceptions of relatively simple aspects of physical reality are mediated by the selectivity of our perception, by our capacity to see what we expect to see, by the theory we have developed about the nature of the world (our cosmology), and by our needs and wishes or our fears and anxieties. It is to a large extent our perception of reality, not reality itself, that influences and determines our behavior.

Consider the behavior of man as it was influenced until the end of the fifteenth century by his perception of a flat rather than a spherical earth. Consider the differences in behavior between a doctor and a layman. If the layman undertakes to treat himself, his perception of the reality of his own disease will in many instances lead him to adopt a method of treatment quite different from what the doctor would prescribe on the basis of his own more professional perception. Consider the question of equity with respect to the administration of salaries or promotions and the quite different perceptions of management and of workers concerning reality. The effort, time, and money devoted to the development of an appropriate corporate image by some companies today are at least a tacit admission that man responds not to reality directly but to his perception of it.

RATIONAL VERSUS EMOTIONAL MAN

Another important aspect of the nature of human nature from the managerial point of view has to do with the emotional characteristics of behavior and their control. The thoughtful manager today is relatively well informed about at least some of these characteristics of human nature. He accepts the fact that some are unconscious and thus uncontrollable by the individual. He is aware of the general findings in psychosomatic medicine and clinical psychology.

Many managers act, however, as though they believe that man is divisible into two *separate* individuals: (1) a rational person who can operate logically, deal with facts, and reach purely objective conclusions and (2) an emotional person who is blindly irrational, ignores or misinterprets facts, and operates in a highly biased fashion. Managers, of course, desire to deal with the former "person" and to exclude the influence of the latter. The ability to make the separation, it is assumed, rests in part on the individual's education and intellectual skills, but primarily on the exercise of will power and the conscious intention to be rational. This ability is believed to be particularly characteristic of the few.

Thus, the tacit belief, reflected in much managerial behavior, is that at least some men can become, if they choose, rational, logical decision-making machines with respect to business problems. Verbal persuasion is usually applied to make man over into this kind of machine: "Let's keep personalities out of this"; "Let's deal with the facts"; "Consider the problem coldly and objectively." If man can only be persuaded to make the attempt, he can largely eliminate from his thinking or behavior the influences of his needs, fears, wishes, anxieties, hostilities, and guilts.

This conception of the nature of man is sharply challenged by the evidence from the psychological clinic and by a considerable body of experimental research. Except possibly for the most trivial acts, man's behavior—whether he is thinking, analyzing, reasoning, or interacting with others—is *always* influenced significantly by emotional factors. He is aware of some of these but not of many others. Generally speaking, the more important the problem or issue under consideration is to him, the greater the influence of emotional factors on his responses. Others cannot eliminate these influences by giving orders or making requests, nor can he eliminate them in himself by the conscious, willful effort to do so. *The emotional and the rational aspects of man are inextricably interwoven; it is an illusion to believe they can be separated.*

A massive body of physiological and psychological evidence supports this generalization. For example, there are specific, differentiated patterns of response of the autonomic nervous system and the glandular system (which are only to a slight degree under conscious control) associated with different kinds of activity. These physiological subsystems are known to be closely tied to emotional reactions.

The rate of heartbeat, the blood pressure, the electrical conductivity of the skin vary measurably and systematically depending on the behavior in which the organism is involved.

The relationships are exceedingly complex, but there is tentative evidence that heart rate *accelerates* somewhat as an individual prepares to undertake a problem-solving task in which he will use his intellectual abilities and knowledge. It accelerates still more as he engages in the task. On the other hand, the heart rate decelerates when he prepares for and later engages in observing, in taking in information from his environment. Moreover, there are significant physiological differences, for example, between an activity associated with "anger toward peers" and one associated with "anger at mother." The subjects are unaware of these differences.

It is well known today that activities in the central nervous and glandular systems can modify the receptivity of sense organs. The accelerated heartbeat rate, as man engages in mental activities of certain kinds, appears to be part of a physiological pattern that partially shuts out certain kinds of stimulation from the environment, while deceleration of the heartbeat is connected with a lowering of the barriers to inputs. Beyond this, to find differential changes associated with reactions to "peers" as opposed to reactions to "mother" is indeed significant.[7]

The important implication for our purposes, from this rapidly growing body of research knowledge, is that emotional responses, many of which are completely unconscious, are associated with virtually all human behavior. It is clear that attempts to eliminate them by verbal persuasion are futile.

A careful study of performance reviews in a division of a large manufacturing company led to a conclusion consistent with these generalizations. It is virtually impossible within the content of the conventional appraisal interview for a superior to communicate a negative evaluation of a subordinate's performance to him without producing defensive reactions. The more severe the criticism (as perceived by the sub-

[7] H. F. Harlow, "The Affectional System in Monkeys," *The American Psychologist*, January, 1962.

ordinate), the more the defensiveness. Thus, the subordinate does not react rationally to the facts. He fails to hear them, or he misinterprets them, or he rejects them as untrue. Much as he may wish to do so, he cannot in these circumstances turn himself into a rational machine. In consequence, changes in behavior attributable to requests by superiors in the context of the appraisal interview turned out in this study to be few indeed.[8]

Human beings in relationships that involve differences in power and status are particularly vulnerable to the effects of emotional forces (note the example above concerning peers versus mothers). The highly sensitive nature of these relationships in childhood and adolescence creates lasting tendencies to react emotionally as well as rationally to them. There are, for example, always subtle and sometimes obvious changes in a subordinate's behavior when he deals directly with those above him in the managerial hierarchy.

It is true that the individual may gain some control over emotional factors influencing his own behavior if he can accept his feelings as facts. If he can come to recognize them, to understand something of the circumstances that arouse them, to accept them as inevitable and integral aspects of his behavior, he can control to some extent their effects.

The process of gaining control over undesired emotional reactions in this fashion is greatly aided if it is one of social interaction. An obvious reason is that, under proper circumstances, the interaction can aid in the recognition of the existence of unconscious emotional reactions and in the discovery of the conditions that arouse them. This is well recognized in everyday life. We seek help along these lines from many sources—from friends, relatives, consultants, colleagues, ministers, psychiatrists. There are tremendously valuable possibilities of achieving more rational business decisions if we can accept certain wider implications of the relationship between social interaction and control of emotional influences on behavior.

A top executive calls a meeting of some of his associates to discuss an important policy decision. Most—perhaps all—of the participants will

[8] E. Kay, H. H. Meyer, and J. R. P. French, Jr., "Effects of Threat in a Performance Appraisal Interview," *Journal of Applied Psychology*, vol. 49, no. 5, pp. 311–317, 1965. H. H. Meyer, E. Kay, and J. R. P. French, Jr., "Split Roles in Performance Appraisal," *Harvard Business Review*, January-February, 1965, pp. 123–129.

be affected by the outcome. It is inevitable, therefore, that emotional influences will be operative. It is clear that ignoring them, or trying to banish them by verbal magic, will not eliminate them. Why not, then, attempt to neutralize them by openly accepting their presence and utilizing the process of social interaction for their control? *We are considerably more capable of detecting the presence of emotional influences in the behavior of others than we are in ourselves.* It is not necessary to engage in psychotherapy or to probe into the causes of such emotional influences in order to compensate reasonably well for them, provided there is recognition of what they are. A group of individuals can help one another to recognize and accept them as facts and in so doing can remove or reduce the very barriers which stand in the way of rational, objective decisions.

We say that an important reason for group consideration of important decisions is to get the benefit of different points of view. Yet by denying or suppressing the emotional factors *which are among the major causes of different points of view*, we defeat our stated purpose.

It is well recognized in everyday life that the effectiveness of social interaction in improving control over emotional influences depends profoundly on the nature of the relationship between the parties involved. It would be critical, therefore, to the success of a strategy such as I am suggesting that the relationships between the members of the group be of a certain kind. Moreover, there are obviously skills involved in successful interaction of this kind. There is good evidence that these skills can be acquired by most normal people. We shall examine such considerations in some detail in Chapters 10 and 11.

It is perhaps not too difficult for the manager to give lip service to these findings about the emotional nature of man. Many do. To include them genuinely in his view of reality so that they become part of the basis for his actions is another matter. The manager is also an example of rational-emotional human nature. His own feelings—partly conscious and partly unconscious—exert important influence on his ability to accept fully that man is not separable into a rational being and an emotional one. To accept the implications of the fact would, for example, alter considerably his view of what is predictable and controllable in the organizational reality that surrounds him.

An important aspect of the lives of forty-five to fifty Sloan Fellows during the year they spend at M.I.T. in the Executive Development

Program is the organization of their own social activities. Since their families move with them to the Boston area for the year, and since they are quite different as a group from the other students at M.I.T., they tend to do many things together.

The management of their extracurricular activities is entirely up to the group. Experience indicates that if they leave these matters to chance, they are likely to lose kinds of control that most of them consider important. They become "managed" by implicit norms and standards that develop in any organization unless explicit attention is given to them.

These matters received rather full discussion in the initial phases of the program for a recent group of Sloan Fellows. The discussion took place in subgroups of a dozen men each. Afterward, in a general session, the suggestion was made and adopted that each subgroup select two representatives to meet together to explore these issues further, preparatory to dealing with them formally. The subgroups then met to select their representatives.

In one group, which I observed, there were clearly different feelings about the issues involved and about the task of choosing representatives. These, however, were ignored, and the suggestion of one member that they select their representative by secret ballot was immediately accepted. Then the suggestion was made that people might feel quite different about the importance of this problem, that some would welcome the opportunity to serve as representatives whereas others would resent being chosen. The group then encouraged individual members to express their feelings. Because the power relationships were negligible (the group consisted of peers), several members did so. It became apparent that, out of twelve, six felt that the issues were trivial, that they had more important things to do and would therefore much prefer not to be chosen. Three others were relatively neutral and would serve willingly if asked. Three, for various reasons, expressed interest in the issues and a genuine desire to have the opportunity to join the "task force."

With this knowledge the group then proceeded to the secret ballot. Two of the three who had expressed a desire to serve were elected.

This was not a critical managerial decision obviously. The consideration of emotional factors, however, influenced the result materially. What impressed me was that if the issue had been genuinely important, it is more likely that feelings would have been denied, ignored, or suppressed in the making of the decision. In this particular case, the implementation of the decision (the work of the task force) might not have been materially affected by the presence of representatives who disliked the task. If the issue had been important, it is not hard to imagine that the implementation desired would have been far less than optimal.

Some of my academic colleagues are fond of saying that emotion is a dirty word in management's lexicon. This is a pointed and largely accurate description. A less colorful but equally correct statement is that management appears to want to eliminate the effects of emotion on behavior in the organizational setting. To the extent that this objective were to be achieved, the organization would reduce its ability to survive!

The essential difficulty is that the typical managerial view of emotion is highly restricted. It ignores the fact that human loyalty, enthusiasm, drive, commitment, acceptance of responsibility, and self-confidence are all emotional variables. So are all the "values we hold dear." Motivation is an *emotional* force. Moreover, the evidence grows that intellectual creativity (as well as artistic creativity) is a process involving emotional factors. Clearly, management does not desire to eliminate these characteristics of human nature from its own or its employees' behavior. In fact, if a human being existed who was completely unemotional, objective, and logical, he would by definition have no *interest* in the success of any organization. He would not be motivated.

The real desire of the manager is that human beings (particularly those with whom he must interact) should express certain emotions and suppress others. He would like to eliminate such emotional characteristics as antagonism, hostility, resistance, defiance, un-cooperative attitudes, and unrealistic points of view. He would like to eliminate emotional forces that are associated in his mind with bad, selfish, immature, and unreasonable behavior. (In fact, many of these are at least partly unconscious and therefore are precisely those which cannot be eliminated by conscious intent.)

A cultural factor is also involved in these implicit desires. The model of the successful manager in our culture is a masculine one. The good manager is aggressive, competitive, firm, just. He is not feminine; he is not soft or yielding or dependent or intuitive in the womanly sense. The very expression of emotion is widely viewed as a feminine weakness that would interfere with effective business processes. Yet the fact is that all these emotions are part of the human nature of men and women alike. Cultural forces have shaped not their existence but their acceptability; they are repressed, *but this does not render them inactive.* They continue to influence attitudes, opinions, and decisions.

It can be stated with some assurance that emotions will influence behavior, including thinking, reasoning, and decision making, whenever they are aroused. Second, they will be aroused to the degree that the issue or problem is important. Third, importance is a function of the (conscious or unconscious) meaning of the issue or the problem or the situation *to the individual*. One of the potential values of the outside consultant in certain situations is that he is more likely to be neutral so far as his emotional involvement in the issues is concerned. However, this is by no means always true. Often the issues, and his role in the resolution of them, are genuinely important to the consultant although for reasons different from those affecting the client.

It is possible for objective reality to be so coercive that the effects of emotional factors upon behavior become negligible, at least for the moment. Thus the "facts" can sometimes determine a decision completely, although the subsequent implementation of the decision may be substantially affected positively or negatively by emotional influences. It is rare, however, for a managerial decision of more than trivial significance to be completely determined by the facts. Even when the facts appear to be coercive, there is usually room for doubt concerning their interpretation or their veracity. Scientific findings are the subject of frequent and sometimes bitter dispute on this score, despite the elaborate safeguards characteristic of scientific methods.

Complete objectivity is a rare phenomenon unless the issues are of little consequence to the individual. This is not to deny the possibility of some gain in striving for it. The general implication from behavioral science knowledge is that man is *by nature* an inseparable mixture of rational and emotional components. He cannot turn himself into a rational "machine" by any known means, nor can he eliminate the effects of emotion on intellectual activity in others by persuasion or by command. He can, however, under certain conditions, utilize the help of others to reduce or compensate for the effects of emotion on their own behavior.

SOCIAL MAN

It is hardly necessary to call attention to the degree to which our society stresses the values of individualism. We have done so for three and a half centuries. Negative attitudes toward conformity, dislike of being "other-directed," carefully contrived legal protection of individual rights, certain attitudes toward government—all reflect these values. The manager, as a member of our society, tends to share them. Thus he stresses the desirability of dealing with individuals as he carries out his managerial responsibilities, for he thinks of the individual as the primary (and only) unit of organized human effort, and of competition between individuals as a major source of motivation.

Of course, complete individual freedom in organizational life is impossible. A degree of control and standardization of individual behavior is obviously necessary. Nevertheless, the manager tends to respond negatively to what he is likely to perceive as "collectivization," whether in the form of face-to-face work groups or in the form of a union. Oddly, he doesn't frown on teamwork, perhaps because he doesn't perceive the team as a collective. I suspect that usually teamwork merely means cooperation between people without reference to an entity called a "team." (Of course, this view of reality has its emotional aspects, whether or not they are recognized. The manager's power may be appreciably affected, depending on whether he deals with individuals or with groups.)

In many cases, the manager's cosmology includes the view that a group is an inefficient means for getting work done, particularly when it comes to activities like planning, decision making, innovating, and problem solving. It is in the nature of human nature, as he views it, that intellectual activities in particular are properly individual activities and are therefore impaired by being carried on in a group. There is much in experience and everyday observation to support this belief. By and large, groups, committees, and task forces *are* grossly inefficient in these respects. Again, however, the question arises whether these are *inherent* characteristics of group activity—unchangeable human nature—or whether they are the *result* of the way groups are managed.

In the last few years, there has been some change in this aspect of managerial cosmology. Formal educative processes designed to improve understanding and skill with respect to group activity have had an impact. The controversy concerning the individual versus the group is by no means settled, but the complexity of reality in a modern industrial organization is gradually producing a reluctant acceptance of the view that groups are appropriate for some kinds of managerial activity. Nevertheless, most managers perceive human nature fundamentally in terms of individual nature. Individual man is the unit of society and of all its organizations.

But man is a social organism, too, and recent studies indicate a close evolutionary relationship between man's emotional and social nature. Knowledge in this field has increased dramatically in recent years, partly as a result of the development of techniques in physiology that permit observation of relationships between behavior and the precise stimulation of certain areas of the brain in living animals (and to a limited extent in man). Also, surgical removal of portions of the brain result in behavior changes, which have been extensively studied.

One region of the mammalian brain is associated with patterns of behavior related to functions like eating and swallowing and to fighting, searching, and self-defense—activities concerned with self-preservation. A related region is associated with grooming reactions and preliminary sexual responses—activities concerned with sustaining the species rather than the self. The latter portion of the nervous system is not found below the level of mammals and is most highly developed in man.[9]

A variety of other findings, coupled with the results of anthropological research, point quite definitely to the conclusion that evolution has been a process not only of competition but of cooperation and mutual support. As one ascends the evolutionary ladder, altruism, idealism, generosity, admiration, and behavior stemming from emotions such as these (which affect survival of the *species*) are gradually added to the more primitive emotions of hostility and acquisitiveness (which affect survival of the *individual*). As one researcher phrased it, "In the complex organization of the old and new structures [of the brain] we presumably have a neural ladder . . . for ascending from the most primitive sexual feeling to the highest level of altruistic sentiments."[10]

Many developments have led to modifications and refinements in evolutionary theory. Although adaptation as a result of natural selection is still a cornerstone of the theory, it is recognized today that natural selection favors the reproductive success of a *population* and that alone. Survival of the individual is irrelevant. A set of conclusions concerning results of a synthesis of findings from several behavioral science disciplines includes the following:

[9] P. H. Knapp (ed.), *The Expression of the Emotions in Man.* New York: International Universities Press, Inc., 1963.
[10] P. D. Maclean, "Phylogenesis," in *ibid.,* p. 32.

Individuals seek and find gratifying those situations that have been highly advantageous in survival of the species. That is, tasks that must be done (for species survival) tend to be quite pleasurable; they are easy to learn and hard to extinguish. Their blockage or deprivation leads to tension, anger, substitutive activity and (if prolonged) depression. Such blockage is often accompanied by emergency-type physiological responses that support actions necessary to correct the situation. In the post-infancy human, a remarkable variety of coping behavior may be mobilized by such blockage or deprivation, determined in substantial part by cultural patterning.[11]

Man is by nature committed to social existence, and is inevitably, therefore, involved in the dilemma between serving his own interests and recognizing those of the group to which he belongs. Insofar as this dilemma can be resolved, it is resolved by the fact that man's self-interest can best be served through his commitment to his fellows. . . . Need for positive effect means that each person craves response from his human environment. It may be viewed as a hunger, not unlike that for food, but more generalized. Under varying conditions it may be expressed as a desire for contact, for recognition and acceptance, for approval, for esteem, or for mastery. . . . As we examine human behavior, we find that persons not only universally live in social systems, which is to say they are drawn together, but also universally act in such ways as to obtain the approval of their fellow men.[12]

Finally:
The available evidence strongly indicates that, throughout the long course of his evolution, man has been a group-living form. Moreover, it is very likely that *the human group,* throughout the history of the species, *has been a powerful problem-solving tool, coping with all sorts of harsh and taxing environmental contingencies.* It has been an adaptive mechanism *par excellence.*[13] (Italics mine.)

One would expect to find evidence supporting these conclusions in the context of organized human effort in industry, and this is what we do find. The classic studies by the Harvard researchers at the Hawthorne works of the Western Electric Company in the late 1920s are a major case in point.[14] The studies of William Foote Whyte on incentive systems,[15] the evidence accumulated by the

[11] D. A. Hamburg, "Emotions in the Perspective of Human Evolution," in *ibid.,* p. 312.
[12] *Ibid.,* p. 308.
[13] *Ibid.,* p. 309.
[14] F. J. Roethlisberger and W. J. Dickson, *Management and the Worker.* Cambridge, Mass.: Harvard University Press, 1939.
[15] W. F. Whyte et al., *Money and Motivation.* New York: Harper & Row, Publishers, Incorporated, 1955.

Institute for Social Research at the University of Michigan,[16] the work of Kurt Lewin and his successors,[17] and many other studies have served to extend and refine knowledge about group behavior.

Both extrinsic and intrinsic rewards and punishments are associated with man's social needs. He needs not only to receive acceptance, support, and recognition in group settings, but also to give these rewards to fellow members. In giving, the rewards are inherent in the action; they are intrinsic. Their evolutionary base is suggested above.

Under appropriate conditions, the group can also be a setting within which the individual satisfies many of his most important ego needs, including those for learning, autonomy (despite a common belief to the contrary), leadership, and self-fulfillment.

A view of reality that ignores or denies these possibilities for goal achievement, or that sees them as inherently incompatible with organizational objectives and requirements, is greatly limited with respect to the managerial task of motivating people to work. Moreover, the theory cited above would suggest that when these social needs are thwarted, individuals will retaliate with aggressive behavior (such as beating the system) and with strong attempts to recreate situations in which needs are met. Evidence and experience in the industrial sphere support this idea: The formation of informal face-to-face work groups, and their powerful influence, is not accidental when management coercively adopts a strategy of dealing exclusively with individuals.

It is important to recognize that the growth of behavioral science knowledge about groups has not resulted in the conclusion that it is necessary to *choose* between the individual and the group. Just as in the physical sciences, understanding of the phenomena at different levels is necessary for prediction and control. The physical particle exhibits properties that are replicated in the atom, in the molecule, and even in a planetary system. However, there are also properties that are unique to each level, and our ability to control natural phenomena is increased by knowledge of the properties of physical systems at different levels.

[16] R. Likert, *New Patterns in Management.* New York: McGraw-Hill Book Company, 1961; and R. Kahn et al., *Organizational Stress.* New York: John Wiley & Sons, Inc., 1964.
[17] R. Lippitt et al., *The Dynamics of Planned Change.* New York: Harcourt, Brace & World, Inc., 1958.

The same is true of human behavior. We study characteristics of cells, of organs, of the nervous system as a whole, of the human being as an organism, of groups, and of larger aggregations of human beings. Certain characteristics are common to all these "systems"; others are unique to each level. Water, for example, is composed of atoms of hydrogen and oxygen. Knowledge about these at the level of the atom would not give us knowledge of the properties of water, nor of the fact that water at temperatures below 32 degrees Fahrenheit becomes solid and floats.

Management's insistence that the individual is the unit of organization is as limiting as an engineer's insistence that the atom is the unit of physical systems. The limitations of a physical technology based on knowledge at one level alone would be great indeed. A molecule is an assembly of atoms, to be sure, but certain *relationships* among the atoms result in molecules with given properties, whereas other relationships result in molecules with entirely different properties. These properties of molecules cannot be predicted solely on the basis of knowledge of the properties of atoms.

Considerations of a similar nature lead the behavioral scientist to question many managerial assertions about the inherent characteristics of human groups. These assertions are based almost entirely on attempts to deal with groups in terms of knowledge of individuals. The accumulated behavioral science knowledge about *group* behavior tends to contradict the idea that the properties of groups are inherently or inevitably those which we typically observe when we deal with groups as mere collections of individuals. It is also demonstrably possible to create relationships between individuals comprising a face-to-face group such that the group exhibits properties almost diametrically opposed to those observed in the typical committee or staff group or task force in everyday organizational life.

Such groups *do* make decisions that are effectively implemented without the necessity for external pressure or surveillance. They are creative and innovative; they operate efficiently; they are not crippled by disagreements or hampered by dominant personalities. Pressures for conformity are minimal, and the knowledge and skills of each member are effectively utilized. The outputs of the group are not mediocre least-common-denominator compromises, but can often yield decisions and problem solutions at a general level of performance superior to the sum of the outputs of the individual members operating separately. Finally, the members perceive the group to be a setting within which there are attractive opportunities to achieve many of their individual goals and to gain intrinsic rewards while *at the same time* contributing to the goals of the organization.

The characteristics of such effective groups will be considered in later chapters, as well as some practical considerations with respect to their development. For the moment, the essential point is that a managerial cosmology limited to "man the individual" excludes important possibilities of improved organizational effectiveness.

SUMMARY

The manager's view of reality exerts profound effects upon his every managerial act. His acts in turn affect the achievement of both his own goals and those of the organization of which he is a member. I have suggested so far a few important ways in which some common managerial perceptions of reality differ from present-day behavioral science knowledge about that reality. These have had to do with the nature of man: how he is motivated, the role of emotion in his behavior, and the significance of his social nature.

It will be fruitful now to consider other aspects of the manager's reality—his view of the industrial organization and his understanding of his own behavior, his identity, and his role. Then we will be in a position to examine, practically, some of the ways in which management styles and strategies might be altered if a view of reality consistent with these behavioral science findings were to be adopted, and what consequences this might have for the achievement of the manager's and the organization's goals.

2

the manager's view of the organization

THE LOGIC OF ORGANIZATIONAL STRUCTURE

One map of a portion of reality upon which managers have relied for many decades is the organization chart and its associated set of position descriptions. This map represents the organization as a structure of responsibilities and a structure of authority. The logic for viewing organizational reality this way is persuasive, and the tendency, therefore, has been to accept this map as a good representation of reality.

The familiar view is that, in a small company, the president (who may also be the owner) carries on all managerial functions. With growth of the firm, some division of labor becomes necessary. Consequently, the president hires other managers to whom he assigns responsibilities for certain parts of the total function. However, in doing so, he retains the overall responsibility for the organization, even though he no longer carries on all the managerial activities.

As the organization grows, each of these subdivisions of responsibility may be further divided, but with the same conception that each manager retains responsibility for everything that is assigned to him from above. He can delegate some of this authority, but he cannot delegate his responsibility. Each managerial position on the chart thus depicts what a man is responsible for, although not necessarily what he does.

Such subdivisions may take many forms. Thus, we have maps of organizations that are functional, or that are organized by product or geographically, or that are organized in terms of some combination of these. We have divisions and departments and smaller work units. One favored conception today is the "profit center," in which most if not all of the managerial functions for a given product or group of products are assigned to a unit headed up by a man who is himself much like the president of a small organization and who is responsible for the financial profitability of his center.

To ensure the fulfillment of these responsibilities and to enable coordination of the parts, there is a structure of authority. The manager of each part, beginning with the smallest, is responsible upward to the manager of the next larger part, and he has authority downward within defined limits over his subdivision. From the bottom up, therefore, there are a chain of responsibility and a chain of command. In order to keep responsibilities clear, each man must have one boss who has authority over him and to whom he is responsible.

Some functional divisions are designed to provide help, advice, and service to the line organization. Managers of such functions have authority only within their functions. The head of each such function is again responsible to one boss in the line organization. There are many variations on this aspect of the map, and certain qualifications are sometimes felt to be necessary. For example, a staff manager in a subdivision of a major organization may report "functionally" to the staff manager at headquarters, but "operationally" to the manager of the subdivision.

Since it seems obvious that man cannot fulfill his responsibilities effectively if he has too many people reporting directly to him, the concept of span of control is invoked. When the number of subordinates reporting directly to a given manager is felt to be unreasonably large, the organization is modified by creating additional levels or subdivisions as necessary.

Thus we have a map of the organization, constructed from a series of positions, which defines a structure of responsibility and a structure of positions. It tells who interacts with whom in terms of command or compliance. In addition, the necessary policies and procedures are formulated to define the interrelationships involved (i.e., the "controls" for making the structure operational). This map is essentially static, in that changes can be effected only by a formal reorganization of these relationships. Minor adjustments to individual positions, of course, can and do occur without reorganization.

THE REALITY OF ORGANIZATIONAL LIFE

The thoughtful manager recognizes today that this map is only a very rough approximation of reality at best. It is a formal picture of the organization, of the way things are *supposed* to be. It is important for placing people in positions, for resolving conflicts, for issuing orders, and for evaluating performance. Obviously, however, managerial activities do not coincide completely with the map. There are many ways of getting things done outside the formal channels or organization, and these are used regularly.

It is also obvious that, despite the logical requirement for it, authority never in fact fully equals responsibility. The manager at any level of the organization is held accountable for things that he cannot directly control, even if he has the formal right to do so. Further, it is clear that staff people do more than merely give advice and help, that they exert powerful influences amounting to authority, although not defined as such. Nevertheless, the chart, the position descriptions, and the associated policies do give a kind of order to a reality that would otherwise be too complex to grasp.

Some managers, most often in smaller organizations, resist the idea of the formal organization chart. What one usually finds, however, is resistance to its *public* use. There may be a chart, kept in the president's desk, often known about but seldom seen by others.

Many reasons are given for keeping the map of the organization private. Among them is the belief that it may serve to limit too much the acceptance of responsibility at various levels. Managers will protect themselves by staying safely within their own limits. Another argument is that such a formal chart may promote quarrels between managers or may permit important responsibilities to "fall down the cracks" between the defined limits. Thus, the formal chart is felt to promote bureaucratic rigidity rather than flexibility.

While these reasons have much truth, there are other less often expressed reasons that may also play a part. A formal organization chart with its accompanying position descriptions clearly limits the power of the manager in the sense that it denies him the possibility of being arbitrary in the demands that he makes on his subordinates. His freedom is restricted, and the ease of changing the organization is likewise restricted. The belief also exists that people will work harder if they are uncertain about what is expected of them and that competition in a somewhat uncertain situation will in the end enable the best men to survive. Thus one often hears the phrase: "Let them work it out among themselves." This conception is essentially the Darwinian one of struggle for survival. (It is not surprising that the associated view of the management organization as a "jungle" often accompanies such a concept of reality.)

The conventional theory of organization is part of a cosmology that includes also a mechanical, rational, and individualistic conception of man. It is a way of bringing order out of chaos, and thus it serves an important function. It is true that human effort must be organized to accomplish the role assigned to industry by society. This organizational theory asserts that *organized* human effort could not exist if human beings were not placed in certain relationships, told what to do, directed, and controlled. The guiding principles for doing these things—authority, responsibility, chain of command, staff and line, span of control, etc.—are eminently logical provided one accepts the premises about the nature of man. However, it is precisely in this respect that the whole conception can be challenged.

If man is not what conventional organization theory assumes him to be, then much of the organization planning carried on within the framework of that theory is nothing more than a *game of logic*. The organization chart, the position descriptions, and the control policies all become an elaborate, formal way of stating what people would do *if* human nature were what it is believed to be.

What we find when we study human behavior in organizations is that people do not behave in everyday organizational life the way the logical theory says they should behave. We discover the existence of an *informal* organization, and study of this shows us what people *are* doing: they are *violating* the conventional principles of organization constantly, and in a great many ways.

Conventional theory asserts that people will behave as individuals in terms of competitive self-interest. They don't. They create informal alliances—cooperative groups—sometimes to further organizational goals (e.g., project teams), and sometimes to defeat them (e.g., work groups under individual incentive plans). Melville Dalton, in his book *Men Who Manage*,[1] presents impressive evidence, obtained from direct observation of middle-level managers, of the informal ways in which cooperative relationships are established to *circumvent* the formal organizational requirements. Many, but not all, of these are ways of getting the job done *in spite of* what these managers perceive as hampering formal requirements.

Conventional theory asserts that each individual is responsible to only one boss. In practice, bosses expect and get compliance from people beside and below them in the organization who are not formally responsible to them. The production foreman does not disregard the informal demands of industrial engineers, maintenance managers, the sales organization, personnel, or accounting—even though they have no formal authority over him—because he knows he could not get his work done or survive in the organization if he

[1] New York: John Wiley & Sons, Inc., 1959.

tried to live within the formal chain of command. This phenomenon of adjusting behavior to conform to the expectations of a variety of peers or superiors is observable at every level of every formal organization I have ever observed. It is the natural human response to role pressure.

Conventional theory states that authority will equal responsibility, and logically this is a necessary corollary of the theory. It isn't true of any manager (including presidents) I have ever known. Every one of them has been held formally accountable for things he could not possibly control. Some of the more successful ones have simply ignored the formal limitations and gone ahead to do what they knew would further organizational goals. They are usually known to top management as the men who "get things done," but there is little open acknowledgment of the fact that they often do so by violating the logical requirements of the formal organization.

I could go on, but I doubt that it is necessary. Any experienced manager can extend and elaborate the basic point: *Human beings in organizations do not behave the way conventional organization theory says they should.* In fact, it would not, in any sense, be an exaggeration to assert that any large organization would come to a grinding halt within a month if all its members began behaving strictly in accordance with the structure of responsibility and authority defined by the formal organization chart, the position descriptions, and the formal controls.

WHY DOES THE GAME OF LOGIC PERSIST?

Why then do we persist in playing this elaborate, unrealistic game? Why do we pretend that reality is what we know it is not? There are undoubtedly many reasons, but one of the important ones, I believe, is the anxiety that man experiences when he cannot perceive order and predictability in his world. The manager who is head of a large and complex organization (from a division level on up) requires a fairly simple and orderly conception of the nature of that organization and of its way of working. Otherwise he could not operate. Conventional organization theory provides him with just such a conception, *and there is no other that is logically as neat or plausible or as readily understandable.* The process of selective perception and memory in combination with his emotional needs enable the manager to *impose* this view on reality even though it is something of a mirage.

The truly fascinating question is: How does it happen that large organizations work as well as they do if the conventional theory is so inconsistent with objective reality? I would offer two reasons. First, there is *some* correlation between the theory and reality. The logic is meaningful, and this conception, since it is quite generally understood, provides at least a rough map for everyone. *Within limits,* people adjust their behavior to it; they act as though it were a true picture.

The second reason is much more important, I believe, and it reflects a deep-seated cultural norm. Those of us who do not become alienated from our society (and that means most of us) accept in a fairly deep and pervasive sense the justice of *reciprocity* in all social relationships. Parents and children accept mutual obligations toward each other; so do buyers and sellers, friends, clients and professional practitioners, citizens and law enforcement agencies. We recognize and accept the fact that unless the tacit obligations of interdependent relationships are at least broadly fulfilled, society itself will break down.

This general acceptance of mutual obligation—the *implicit* social contract—applies equally to the relationships between employer and employee. Underneath all the bickering, the resistance, the indifference toward specific aspects of the relationship is the *accepted* obligation of the employer to provide extrinsic rewards for work and the *accepted* obligation of the employee to provide work in return for rewards. This is what keeps organizations going.

I don't know of formal research studies directed to this phenomenon, but it seems to me the evidence for it in everyday experience is overwhelming. I can think of literally hundreds of examples of behavior at every level of the industrial organizations I have observed which violate to some extent the demands of the *formal* system but which represent clear attempts to achieve organizational goals. A very large proportion of employees—workers and managers alike—accept the implicit obligation of the employment contract to a degree that leads them to try to help the organization succeed *in spite of* restrictions and obstacles imposed by the formal structure and controls.

At the same time many of those same employees will in effect sabotage procedures and regulations that they perceive to be unreasonable or unfair. It is the observation of these forms of behavior that tends to obscure the broader underlying acceptance of the obligations of the employment contract. If that obligation is defined as compliance with management demands in all respects, then there *is* a large amount of indifference and resistance in every large organization. If, on the other hand, the obligation is defined as a broad willingness to contribute effort toward organization goals in return for rewards, then one can argue it is widely accepted.

The general results are that management clings to the conventional principles. Behavior that clearly interferes with organizational success can be corrected, management believes, by their more consistent application. Behavior that "gets things done" is ignored or winked at even if it is in violation of them.

I am inclined to believe that the degree of success achieved by industry is, to a considerable extent, attributable to man's general acceptance of the obligation inherent in the employment contract *in spite of* the difficulties created by application of the formal principles of organization. The value of conventional organization theory is primarily that it serves certain deep emotional needs of management, not that it provides a realistic formula for action. This is a strong statement, and the evidence to prove it is lacking. It has been interesting, however, to discover that many managers at middle and lower levels of organization and many colleagues who have observed organizational behavior clearly agree with it.

There may never be a theory of organization and a set of principles as simple, orderly, and logically persuasive as the one that has been the model during the last half century. One consequence of the growth of scientific knowledge in any field is the necessity to abandon relatively simple conceptions of the nature of reality for more complex and less consistent ones. Paradoxes abound in natural phenomena—physical *and* biological—and theoretical complexity is a frequent consequence of the attempt to resolve them. This problem is particularly acute in the behavioral sciences. Perhaps we should take comfort in the fact that human behavior is not explainable in simple terms. Certainly the more that is learned about it, the less simple it appears to be.

Toward more complexity.   There is a hopeful, but challenging, aspect of this problem, however: Research on creativity suggests that one of the correlates of innovation is the ability, not merely to accept, but to enjoy complexity and apparent disorder![2] The creative genius who will discover a theory of organization to satisfactorily replace the conventional one may some day appear. For the moment, however, we have the choice of accepting a theory that is demonstrably unrealistic and limited or of using as best we can the knowledge that exists, even though it does not add up to a neat and orderly theory. Clearly I have chosen the second alternative.

A SYSTEMS VIEW OF ORGANIZATION

I have argued that the difficulty with many traditional views of reality is not that they are wrong but that they are partial. They are based on necessary but insufficient causes. A similar problem exists with the more traditional views of nature of the organization. It becomes necessary with such a conception to consider all the behavior that is unexplained by the "map" as exceptional behavior. This creates a difficulty because what is not explained turns out to be greater than what is.

There is a growing tendency to describe human organizations within a broad framework of thinking called *general systems theory*.[3] This theory uses certain concepts to gain understanding of a wide range of phenomena in the physical sciences, in biology, and now in the behavioral sciences. These phenomena are common to many different systems, ranging from the atom to the galaxy, from the cell to the organism, from the individual to society. Let us consider what it means to view an industrial organization as a system within this framework.

A system is an assembly of interdependent parts (subsystems) *whose interaction determines its survival*. Interdependence means

---

[2] H. E. Gruber, G. Terrell, and M. Wertheimer (eds.), *Contemporary Approaches to Creative Thinking*. New York: Atherton Press, 1962; H. H. Anderson (ed.), *Creativity and Its Cultivation*. New York: Harper & Row, Publishers, Incorporated, 1959.

[3] *Some of McGregor's colleagues have recently written important basic books in this area: E. H. Schein,* Organizational Psychology. *Englewood Cliffs, N.J.: Prentice-Hall, Inc., 1965; D. Katz and R. L. Kahn,* The Social Psychology of Organizations. *New York: John Wiley & Sons, Inc., 1966. Undoubtedly the work of another close colleague contributed heavily to interest in a systems approach: J. W. Forrester,* Industrial Dynamics. *Cambridge, Mass.: The M.I.T. Press, 1961. (Eds.)*

that a change in one part affects other parts and thus the whole system. Such a statement is true of atoms, molecules, cells, people, plants, formal organizations, and planetary systems.

The choice of subsystems and of the basic unit is to some degree a matter of convenience. In physics, for example, the particle may be the appropriate unit for some purposes, while the atom or the molecule may be appropriate for other purposes. One could, in fact, consider an industrial organization as an assembly of molecules, for it is! In our present state of knowledge, this would not be particularly useful. For practical purposes, then, the unit that is viewed as basic to the human organization is the individual.

As noted above, subsystems at all levels of a major system have properties or characteristics in common. It is also true that each level has certain unique properties, which is, in fact, a criterion for selecting appropriate levels. This is an important consideration, for it means that we may expect to find that the individual human organism, the face-to-face work group, the functional department, the division, and the total organization have unique properties as well as properties in common. If our expectation is fulfilled, it might enable us to understand some of the discrepancies between what conventional organization theory (based entirely on the individual) says behavior *should* be and what we find it is. It is a commonplace of systems theory that the behavior of the whole (at any level) cannot be predicted solely by knowledge of the behavior of its subparts. Conventional organization theory, however, does attempt to predict the behavior of the organization on the basis of assumptions about individuals.

An industrial organization is an *open* system. It engages in transactions with a larger system: society. There are inputs in the form of people, materials, and money and in the form of political and economic forces arising in the larger system. There are outputs in the form of products, services, and rewards to its members. Similarly, the subsystems within the organization down to the individual are open systems.

An industrial organization is an *organic* system. It is adaptive in the sense that it changes its nature as a result of changes in the external system around it. The adaptation, however, is not passive; the system affects the larger system as well as being affected by it. It copes with its environment as the individual human being copes with his. It is dynamic in the sense that it undergoes constant change as a result of interaction among the subsystems and with the larger environmental system.

Finally, an industrial organization is a *sociotechnical* system. It is not a mere assembly of buildings, manpower, money, machines, and processes. The system consists in the *organization* of people around various technologies. This means, among other things, that human relations are not an optional feature of an organization— they are a built-in property. The system exists by virtue of the motivated behavior of people. Their relationships and behavior determine the inputs, the transformations, and the outputs of the system.

CONCLUSIONS

Thinking about an industrial organization as an open, organic, sociotechnical system has several advantages. One of the major ones is that it can represent reality more fully and more adequately than the conventional picture of the formal organization. It provides a better basis for understanding what does go on rather than what ought to go on. It brings the activities of the informal organization into the framework without excluding those of the formal organization. It enlarges and enriches the possibility of understanding the many complex cause-effect relationships constituting an organization. Thus it promises better prediction and better control. Without becoming highly technical, we shall use the systems way of thinking in later parts of this volume in examining a number of typical organizational phenomena.

Let us go now to consider another equally complex system, the manager himself.

part two

MANAGERIAL
BEHAVIOR

3

the manager's role

Until this point we have been looking at certain universal characteristics of man and at some of the ways in which his behavior is influenced by relationships between these characteristics and those of his work environment. We shall now narrow the focus of attention to the manager. The formula $B = f(I_{a,b,c,}...E_{m,n,o,}...)$ will provide the framework,[1] but our concern will be with the relationships between I variables and E variables that have particular relevance to *managerial* behavior.

THE IDEA OF ROLE

One might say that a manager's role is defined by a position description which states his responsibilities and authority, and a title which locates his position in the organizational hierarchy. In the purely formal sense this is true, but such a definition is a gross oversimplification of reality. The formal position description takes no account of many other influences that define and limit acceptable behavior. Some of these are themselves formal: policies; control procedures (capital-expense budgets, cost accounting, inventory and scheduling, etc.); collective bargaining agreements. Others are informal but equally important. They consist in the *expectations* of others (superiors, subordinates, peers inside the organization, and often outsiders such as vendors, customers, stockholders, government officials) about how the responsibilities of the position will be fulfilled. Together with the position description and the title, these constitute the objective requirements of the role.

We have seen that an individual's perception of reality is influenced by selective processes of many kinds. The manager's behavior—his fulfillment of his role—is therefore not simply the sum of all these objective influences but his synthesis of them. That synthesis is his unique way of resolving the interplay of forces in him with forces in the environment.

The forces in the environment are by no means always explicit or consistent, and the forces within him are by no means purely rational or conscious. Nevertheless, he develops a conception of his role out of his experience, and he behaves in accordance with that

[1] *P was used in Chap. 1 to represent "performance." B is used here as a symbol of "behavior"—the more generic and typical usage. (Eds.)*

conception. The complexity of this process as stated in Chapter 2 should make us wary of the oversimplification embodied in traditional organization charts and position descriptions. Necessary as they may be for some purposes, they are inadequate for understanding the manager's behavior. They are necessary but insufficient causes.

ROLE DEFINITION

A common method for overcoming some of the problems of role definition is for a staff organization specialist to interview a manager at length about what he does, what his responsibilities are, what his relationships are with others. The position description thus obtained is then taken to the manager's superior, who either approves it or modifies it until he is satisfied that it is an accurate statement of what the role should be.

In a study by Norman Maier and two colleagues a number of vice presidents in several organizations were each asked to select an immediate subordinate with whose work they were thoroughly familiar, and to define his role (including major responsibilities, priorities among these, and qualifications required by the job). The subordinates were then requested to define their own roles independently but with respect to the same variables. The agreement between the members of the pairs was of the order of 35 percent.[2]

This degree of agreement was not significantly different in companies that had formal appraisal programs and in companies that did not. One would expect, certainly, that the agreement between managers and subordinates would be higher in the former case because of the periodic discussions of performance that would reveal the superior's expectations to the subordinates.

A number of studies at other managerial levels have consistently revealed marked discrepancies between the superior's views of the role of his immediate subordinates (his expectations) and the subordinate's perception of these expectations.[3] The evidence seems to indicate that the formal procedures of organization planning do

[2] N. R. F. Maier, W. Read, and J. Hooven, "Breakdowns in Boss-Subordinate Communication," in *Communication in Organizations: Some New Research Findings.* Ann Arbor, Mich.: Foundation for Research on Human Behavior, 1959.

[3] R. L. Kahn et al., *Organizational Stress.* New York: John Wiley & Sons, Inc., 1964.

not fulfill their purpose of clarifying roles even when the individual manager "participates" in the process of writing his own position description, nor, apparently, does day-to-day interaction on the job!

Organization planners typically explain findings like these by saying that (1) position descriptions are seldom kept current, and (2) managers don't *use* them, but file them away and forget them. Therefore actual behavior drifts away from the formally defined role.

ROLE CONFLICT

Although both of these statements are true, another explanation is that position descriptions are used very little because the manager typically finds that he cannot fulfill the role that is thrust upon him by the day-to-day exigencies of organizational life and at the same time act consistently with the requirements of his position description. The role pressures arising from the expectations of others make a mockery of the neat, logical, formal statements of what he *should* do.

The director of a major staff department in the headquarters organization of a large company is responsible, according to his position description, for maintaining relations with the field and for ensuring a flow of information into his department that will enable him to recognize problems and foresee trends requiring major changes in company policies relating to his function. He is responsible for recommending such changes to his top management.

In day-to-day practice several of the top executives use this man as an "errand boy" to take care of a great mass of trivial problems that come over their desks. It is rare for him to finish a discussion with a subordinate or to carry through a scheduled staff meeting without being summoned "upstairs" in connection with some minor problem. He is in fact an assistant to these executives and not the head of an important staff department.

He has attempted without success to get his superiors to perceive the consequences of their behavior. They give lip service to his formally defined role but ignore it in practice. Clearly any attempt to rewrite his position description to conform to the absurdities of reality would be unacceptable. Yet these same executives are dissatisfied because they feel that the formal responsibilities assigned to his department are not very well fulfilled. They have agreed privately that he is not a very good administrator and that he has more people than he can handle reporting to him. They plan to insist that he streamline his unit and reduce its size by about 30 percent.

ROLE PRESSURES (F)

Inconsistencies between formal position descriptions and actual role pressures are but one illustration of the many sources of role conflict which most managers experience. Maintenance department managers face constant and intense conflicting pressures from operating departments managers each of whom wants his requirements to be given top priority. Development engineering groups are caught between demands for the completion of projects and what they know will be the pressures if through haste they overlook some feature of design that will create problems when the process or product gets into manufacturing. Members of sales groups are in a role conflict because of customer pressures on the one hand and manufacturing scheduling on the other. Staff groups are often expected to provide advice and help to the line organization, and at the same time to administer control systems which place them in a surveillance role over the very people they are expected to help.

The truly remarkable thing is that managers are able to cope at all successfully with the great array of role pressures. The conflicting role pressures faced by the first-line production supervisors (from superiors, subordinates, union stewards, industrial engineers, accountants, schedulers, etc.) have been extensively studied because of the critical position these supervisors occupy between the work force and management, but problems of role conflict exist everywhere in the managerial hierarchy. The conventional functions of organization planning and role definition tend often to aggravate rather than alleviate these problems.

One particularly aggravating panacea is the concept that "authority equals responsibility." Organization specialists (and many higher-level executives) hide behind this concept by saying of subordinates: "They have the authority to act, but they won't use it." (I have heard this statement made about foremen with respect to their handling of discipline and grievances hundreds of times.) Let us consider the manager's authority more closely.

It is true in only a very circumscribed sense that because a man is a manager he can give an order with the confident expectation that it will be obeyed. Usually he cannot discipline, much less fire, a recalcitrant subordinate without following an elaborate set of formal procedures, and even then not without some risk that his action will be overruled either by his own superiors or by an arbitrator.

The union contract is but one restriction on managerial authority. Unless he is at the very top of his organization, the manager's power will be sharply limited by a variety of managerial control systems including capital and expense budgeting, cost control, scheduling, personnel policies and procedures, industrial engineering procedures, and (from outside the organization) legal restrictions on his freedom to act. In addition to all these formal limitations, he knows that his career as a manager will be affected by what is loosely called his ability in getting along with people, which often means playing a cautious political game rather than utilizing the power that is presumably associated with his position in the managerial hierarchy.

Role pressures also exist in society outside the organization. The impact of these is greatest on top managers who are in the public eye, but it is not absent for any manager in his social interaction on or off the job.

The stereotype of the manager in our society today is inconsistent and ambivalent. On the one hand it includes the view that he has but one responsibility: to contribute to the economic performance of the enterprise. On the other hand it includes the view that management has major social responsibilities in addition to economic ones, not only toward the employees of the enterprise, but toward the community, government, education, charitable enterprises, and the public generally. The manager is respected and admired, yet feared. He has high status, yet he is under constant suspicion of manipulating people (employees, customers, stockholders, the government) for purposes of economic gain or personal power.

ROLE PRESSURES (I)

This brief look at environmental role pressures (E variables) has been illustrative, but by no means exhaustive. The manager's conception of his role—and his ability to occupy it successfully—

depends also on his own characteristics (I variables). Among these are his cosmology, his values, his needs, his capabilities, his view of himself.

The manager's role as a manager is enhanced (and complicated) by the fact that he is also a human being who has developed a set of values. He possesses firm, emotionally based beliefs about what is "good" and "bad" with respect to the religious, political, social, economic, and personal aspects of life. He cannot leave these important characteristics of his personality behind when he goes to work. They are part of his identity. If he cannot reconcile his values with the perceived role pressures of his job, he will be in a conflict that will interfere with his performance either as a manager or as a human being outside of work. Yet the fact is that there are basic conflicts of this sort that appear to be almost impossible to resolve in our society today.

Will he "marry the job" if this involves shirking his responsibilities as a husband and father? Will he become a "servant of the corporation" and rationalize or ignore his own personal values when they conflict with the impersonal, efficiency-dominated, profit-maximization-oriented values of the economic enterprise? Will he play the "political game" that is an inherent part of achieving advancement and recognition in any large industrial enterprise? Will he accept and support decisions and policies made by others which, at least occasionally, are in conflict with his conceptions of fair and just treatment of his fellow human beings?

It is interesting to see how frequently these and similar issues are major preoccupations, if not chronic problems, of managers, particularly for those who have attained a status in their organization where they can afford to take a hard look at their careers. Concern with such issues is quite visible and typical in managers attending management development programs in a university like my own. In addition to the formal reasons for attending such programs, it is clear that they afford an opportunity to examine one's role and to test one's own conclusions against those of others.

If the manager is a top-level executive, the probabilities are high that he has gotten there by demonstrating competence as an operating manager, that is, by dealing successfully with the day-to-day problems of a concrete kind which occupy perhaps three-quarters of the time and attention of middle-level managers.

As a top-level executive, it is unlikely that he will have responsibility for the *direct operation* of anything. His time and attention will be taken up with consideration of problems of an entirely different kind. The relations between the enterprise and the external environment will be critical. Much of his time and energy will be spent in the establishment of broad policies and in planning, assessing the behavior and accomplishment of the enterprise as a whole, and analyzing the causes of inadequate performance. For the former operating manager this is often a most frustrating role.

One large company makes a deliberate attempt to move a selected group of young managers believed to have potential for top executive roles as rapidly as possible through the middle levels of management. The belief is that too much experience at operating levels creates habits and perceptions that are liabilities rather than assets in the performance of top-level executive functions.[4]

PRESSURES OF NEW KNOWLEDGE

The development of scientific knowledge brings pressures to bear upon the manager's perception of his role. One of the most difficult to resolve has to do with the professionalization of management. The systematic and rapid accumulation of knowledge in all the disciplines that have relevance to management is a major phenomenon of our time. Behavioral science knowledge is one example, but others are no less important. Computer technology, applied mathematics, statistics, and symbolic logic, most of which have hitherto been of relatively small concern to the manager, are becoming highly relevant. As industrial firms become international in character, they must acquire additional knowledge in political science, history, anthropology, economics, and perhaps also philosophy and ethics.

Clearly the industrial manager cannot hope to acquire detailed, systematic knowledge in all these fields. Equally clearly, he cannot afford to ignore this knowledge and its implications for managerial strategy and practice. Can he rely on specialists, within his organization or outside it, to ensure that relevant knowledge is brought to bear on the decisions which he makes? If he can, there are addi-

[4] A. T. M. Wilson, "The Manager and His World," *Industrial Management Review*, 1961.

tional questions of how to make use most effectively of the specialists who have this knowledge and can keep abreast of it. How can he make competent judgments about their qualifications and competence; how can he counteract the inevitable narrowness of their view of reality?

Is management becoming a science? Must the manager of the future be himself a scientist? Will intuition and judgment and good common sense and rich experience continue to provide an adequate base for effective management even in the fairly immediate future? Or will these important qualifications cease to have significant value in the face of scientific and technical knowledge aided by the impressive capabilities of the computer?

Thus the very growth of knowledge relevant to management raises profound questions that no manager can ignore. He must somehow come to terms with them in order to determine the nature of his role as a manager.

SELF-ASSESSMENT

The manager's performance in his role is also a function of his assessment of his own capabilities. Again, of course, this is a matter of his perception, not of objective reality. He may overestimate or underestimate the degree of any or all of his capabilities. He also makes subjective evaluation of the *importance* of certain capabilities for the performance of his managerial job. Some managers, for example, place high value on their practical experience. To them, having come up from the bottom of the organization is a critical factor in their present success, and they are likely to insist that it is equally so for others. Some managers place high value on certain kinds of formal education. Alfred P. Sloan, for example, believed that an engineering education contributes in a major way to managerial success.

A manager's assessment of his own capabilities naturally affects the ways in which he relates to others. His acceptance and utilization of certain kinds of staff help will depend on his view of his own areas of expertness. The impact on an organization of its president differs considerably according to the functions of the business in which he believes himself to be most competent. The problems created for the organization by top-level executives who have had long experience in line operations, and who persist in using their skills to make day-to-day operating decisions from a headquarters position, have already been alluded to.

On the other hand, a manager's undervaluation of some of his own capabilities may lead to overdependence on others, unwillingness to take risks, and indecisiveness, or sometimes to insistence that certain capabilities are of little or even negative value to managerial success. This explains the hostility of some "practical" managers toward those whom they regard as too theoretical, or of academically trained managers toward those who "can't understand theory."

Obviously there is no single program or method of organizational planning that will eliminate the difficulties created for every manager by conflicting, unclear, or unintended role pressures. On the contrary, virtually every phase of managerial activity has effects of one kind or another on managerial roles. Each of the chapters that follow deals with aspects of organized human effort which, depending on how they are handled, will affect managerial roles.

Finally, it must be emphasized again that the individual is not a passive agent in the process of determining his role. He does not simply "adjust" to the objective role pressures. He perceives some of them, ignores others, and interprets others in ways that conform to his needs, goals, and attitudes. He makes active attempts to modify some of the role pressures that he perceives to be unreasonable. The process of defining his role is a "transactional" one that is in part conscious and rational but in larger part unconscious and emotionally influenced. Moreover, it is an almost continuous process of trial and error in which there are frequent necessities for redefinition caused by either external or internal changes in "demand."

Formal procedures that ignore or deny this transactional character of role definition do not in fact eliminate it, but simply increase the discrepancy between the formal definition and the reality. Effective organization planning is not something "done to" an organization either by staff or by higher management imposing a particular form on lower parts of the organization. Ideally it is something an organization does to itself through continuous mutual interaction with "consultant help" from staff.

CONCLUSIONS

The role of the manager can be visualized as a dynamic interplay between environmental forces and pressures operating on the manager (the E variables) and forces originating from within the manager, his values, personality, and aspirations (the I variables). Role conflict is inescapable, for there is really no way that a manager can harmonize perfectly the competing pressures emanating from within and from without.

For the professional manager, the magnitude of role conflict is likely to increase in one way, for the environment of the modern manager is more dynamic, turbulent, and clogged than that of his counterpart operating in the relatively stable and more certain world of the nineteenth century. More is expected of him. Not only is he expected to operate an efficient enterprise at a reasonable profit; he is also expected to possess interpersonal competence and extensive skills in a wide variety of management sciences, such as statistics, economics, and linear programming. In another way, the conflict is more bearable precisely because management is emerging as a well-defined profession based on the behavioral and management sciences. The new role of the professional manager, anchored in many disciplines, can help to provide security and continuity in a rapidly changing world.

In any case, the transaction between the external world and the manager's personal identity is complex, abounding in strains and possibilities. Finding a way to cope with tension and to confront and grow from conflict is a genuine challenge. (Eds.)

4

the manager's style

We have examined a number of variables that exert an important influence on the manager's behavior as a manager: his beliefs about the nature of man and about cause-effect in human behavior (his cosmology), his perception of the role pressures that he faces in performing his job, his personal values, his needs, his perception of his own capabilities. All his past and present experience as well as his own biological inheritance have interacted to create the unique person that he is.

Every individual reveals to those who know him well certain predictable patterns of behavior. He tends to respond to environmental pressures with some, although by no means complete, consistency. Taken as a whole, his predictable ways of coping with the reality of the work environment may be termed his *managerial style*.

It is true that every manager's style is unique, but as a part of our characteristic human tendency to group similar phenomena into categories so that we can simplify reality enough to cope with it, we perceive similarities and ignore differences so that we can apply generalized labels. Accordingly, we speak of different managers as being paternalistic, authoritarian, democratic, permissive, "bull of the woods," soft, hard, firm but fair, scientific, production-centered, employee-centered, etc. Thus we categorize similar, but by no means identical, patterns of behavior into managerial styles. Once again, it is our *perception* of reality that enables us to attach these labels to groups of managers. No individual is as completely consistent in his own behavior or as similar to others as the label implies.

Moreover, the label is the result of *our* perceptions of an individual, not his perception of himself. Unconscious forces operating in him may lead him to quite a different perception of himself. He has usually not gone through a conscious, deliberate process of deciding on a certain style. Rather, it has emerged as a result of his lifetime of coping with reality.

HOW STYLES EMERGE AND HOW THEY ARE KNOWN

A useful way of viewing these differences between individuals is provided by the Johari "window"[1] in Figure 1. Some characteristics

[1] J. Luft, "The Johari Window," *Human Relations Training News*, vol. 5, pp. 6–7, 1961.

of an individual's personality are perceived both by him and by others (sector 1). Some are perceived by others but unrecognized by the individual because they are the result of unconscious forces

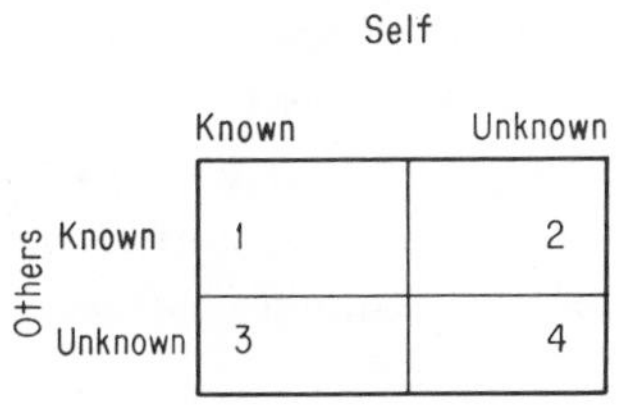

FIGURE 1. The Johari Window. (J. Luft, *Group Processes,* Palo Alto, Calif.: National Press Publications, 1962.)

(sector 2). Some are perceived by the individual but deliberately and successfully hidden from others (sector 3). Finally, there are characteristics which are so deeply buried that neither the individual nor others perceive them, but they nevertheless influence his behavior (sector 4).

In the course of interaction, the individual may choose to reveal things about himself that are unknown to others, thus expanding sector 1 and contracting sector 3. Under some circumstances, others may help an individual to recognize things about himself that they perceive and he does not, thus enlarging sector 1 and contracting sector 2. Sector 4 will remain unchanged without psychotherapy or the development of an unusually intimate personal relationship.

The individual's managerial style is influenced by characteristics in sector 2 (which others perceive but he does not) as well as by characteristics in the other sectors. Thus he and others perceive reality differently, but neither perceives the "actual" reality. Thus also, because of the nature of sectors 2 and 4, an individual's style is rarely completely consistent. We may ignore the inconsistencies if they are not marked; if they are, we find him puzzling, complex, difficult to understand.

Managers also tend to show considerable interest in psychological tests that purport to reveal their style, thus indicating how much style is a product of trial-and-error coping rather than deliberate planning. The Blake Managerial Grid (Figure 2), which determines managerial style on the basis of the individual's perceptions of a number of specific kinds of behavior, is an example.[2] Scoring him-

[2] R. R. Blake and J. S. Mouton, *The Managerial Grid.* Houston, Tex.: Gulf Publishing Company, 1964.

self on each of the test items, the manager is able to *discover* his style! If the process of developing a style were logical, consistent, and conscious, there would be no need for or interest in a test of this kind.

The insights that a manager can gain from the processes of feedback in a T Group[3] are frequently helpful to him in discovering the discrepancies between what he thinks his impact is on others and what in fact it is. Under these "protected" conditions, and if the individual so desires, he can then deliberately modify his own behavior and test it against the perceptions of others in order to make it more consistent with his own desired style.

For many purposes, a grouping of managerial styles into categories broader than those which arise rather spontaneously from everyday experience (like the labels listed above) is useful. Roughly similar cosmologies resulting from widely held beliefs in our society about the nature of man; common economic, political, and social values; and broad similarities in the nature of industrial organizations make it possible to group a fairly sizable majority of managerial styles in the United States today into three categories: hard, soft, and firm but fair.

These labels are in general use among managers today. They underlie the categories used in the Blake Managerial Grid. Common to all three is a relatively heavy reliance on extrinsic rewards and punishments as the means for influencing organized human effort in industry. As I have argued earlier, an implicit mechanical theory of cause and effect has influenced the evolution of these three styles. The first emphasizes extrinsic threat of punishment, the second emphasizes extrinsic rewards; and the third (by far the most common today) recognizes the necessity for balancing rewards and punishments.

There are, of course, many modifications and combinations of these three styles, and there are swings from one to another as external economic, political, and social conditions change.

---

[3] *McGregor refers throughout this volume to the T Group and other NTL-associated learning methods. The interested reader can turn to two recent books on this subject: E. H. Schein and W. G. Bennis,* Personal and Organizational Change through Group Methods: The Laboratory Approach. *New York: John Wiley & Sons, Inc., 1965; and L. P. Bradford, J. R. Gibb, and K. D. Benne,* T-Group Theory and Laboratory Method. *New York: John Wiley & Sons, Inc., 1964. (Eds.)*

THE MANAGERIAL GRID

A provocative theory of the relationships between these managerial styles was developed by Robert Blake and Jane Mouton; they have called it the *grid theory*.[4] Fundamentally, it rests on the proposition that there are two major variables affecting managerial style:

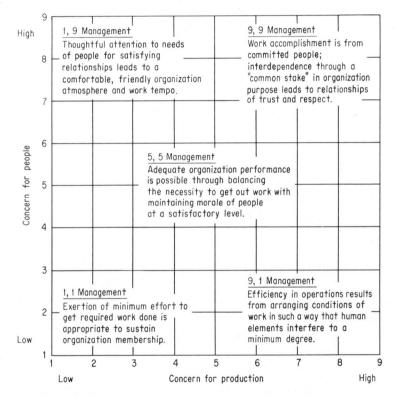

FIGURE 2. The Managerial Grid: Concern For Production. (R. R. Blake and J. S. Mouton, *The Managerial Grid*, Houston, Tex.: Gulf Publishing Company, 1964.)

"concern for production" and "concern for people." By representing these as coordinates on a graph and giving each a range in intensity from 1 to 9, it is possible to chart a wide array of managerial styles (eighty-one possible combinations) with the five predominant ones appearing as shown in Figure 2.

[4] Blake and Mouton, *op. cit.*

There is a position (9, 9) on the grid representing maximum concern for both people and production, which Blake and Mouton call the *team theory of management*. My own view is that a team theory does not evolve simply from the maximization of the two variables represented on the grid. As we have seen, managerial style is the result of complex interaction among *many* variables.[5]

The Managerial Grid does nevertheless provide a useful if much oversimplified view of a variety of managerial styles which are commonly recognized today and which rely primarily on extrinsic rewards and punishments. In fact, I suspect that the majority of managers in American industry would perceive the grid as exhausting the possibilities of managerial style (if we ignore for the moment what Blake and Mouton call team management).

It is obvious that all three of the major styles I mentioned earlier (hard, soft, firm but fair) and many variations and combinations among them do work. The success of our system of enterprise is testimony to this fact. It is also obvious from experience that there are gains and losses in organizational effectiveness associated with each style. The firm-but-fair managerial style is probably perceived by most managers as the optimal form, and it is certainly the most common one.

My argument is that these managerial styles are not as successful as they might be because they have evolved from inadequate cosmologies. The notions of cause and effect on which they are based largely ignore the existence of *intrinsic* rewards and punishments. To a considerable extent also, they fail to recognize the interweaving of man's rational and emotional characteristics and his social human nature.

There are other implications, however, than those of cosmology alone. The acceptance of the existence of intrinsic rewards and punishments, of emotional factors in behavior, and of man as a social being has important implications for the manager's perception of his role. For example, an implication which may seem to him obvious (but which is, in fact, not true) is that his power would be materially reduced if he were to accept the implications for practice inherent in this different cosmology. He could control only indirectly and remotely by means of intrinsic rewards and punishments, whereas he can directly give or withhold extrinsic ones. He could not predict the effects of emotional behavior on the (he

[5] *See Chapter 10 for McGregor's elaboration of "team management."* (*Eds.*)

believes rational) managerial processes of decision making, planning, and organizing. If he were to accept the concept of social man, he would find himself a minority of one (even though he is the leader with primary power) in a group of subordinates who conceivably might "gang up" against him.

THE PROBLEMS OF CHANGE IN MANAGERIAL STYLE

These concerns are more or less openly expressed by managers contemplating the implications of recent behavioral science knowledge. One common form of expression consists in statements like: "Most people want to be dependent and led"; "The necessities of a machine technology prevent the worker from obtaining intrinsic rewards because he is essentially machine-controlled"; "These ideas are merely a dressed-up version of 'permissive' management, and it has already been demonstrated that this doesn't work—groups can't make decisions."

Another reaction is to ignore or minimize the negative side effects of existing managerial styles and to magnify the problems that would occur if a different style were to be adopted.

To suggest, even in a roundabout fashion, that a manager's style is inadequate tends to be threatening. The reasons are obvious if we realize how deeply rooted his style is in his fundamental beliefs, his values, his perception of himself, and his lifetime of experience. The manager may be quite willing to alter specific and superficial "tactical" habits, but it is another matter to expect him to change in more basic ways.

I believe that this is one of the reasons for the expressed concern about whether certain management training programs are attempts to change personality. In fact they *are* to the degree that they are concerned with managerial style in the way the term is used here. Many conventional forms of management training are attempts to get managers to adopt a certain style that is felt by training directors or higher levels of management to be desirable.

Such programs would seem threatening to many were it not that there is a relatively easy out. The trainee can, and often does, change his *perception* of his own style without in fact changing his basic beliefs and values. In doing so, he is not necessarily making a deliberate attempt to deceive others, but is often using a protective device involving unconscious forces. He can, however, rationalize this process.

The manager may believe quite sincerely that he has changed his style when in fact he has merely interpreted and modified what he has learned so that he can assimilate it to the style he brought with him into the program. The point is that because a manager's style is profoundly influenced by his cosmology and his identity, any significant change will occur only if these underlying causal systems are altered. This usually requires much more than listening to lectures, reading books, discussing cases, and the like.

Another illustration of the same phenomenon is often observable in an organization when management wishes to decide whether to adopt an innovation in the form of a new policy or procedure that is being discussed in managers' circles or has been described in a management journal. One of the most common initial steps is to send people to other companies to see what they are doing. It is usually recognized that a program or policy or procedure cannot simply be lifted out of the context of one company and placed unchanged in another company. The common phrase is, "We will adapt it to our situation."

It can be predicted with fair certainty that the process of "adaptation" will be one of assimilation to the style already characteristic of the adapting organization. When the differences in style are not great, such adaptations may be fairly successful. When the differences are substantial, the adaptation process is likely to fail.

A few years ago I published an article about performance appraisal that raised some questions about the managerial cosmology that underlies many conventional systems.[6] A few companies, recognizing and agreeing with the implications of that article, have since attempted some fundamental changes in their managerial style and as a result have evolved a variety of technical innovations (i.e., programs and procedures). When they have succeeded in bringing about changes in style, they have been quite satisfied with the results.

The significant changes, however, were not at the procedural level. These were indications of a much deeper change from a conception of managing based on telling subordinates what to do, supervising their doing of it, and then telling them how well they have done it to one based on *joint* planning and goal setting, helping the subordinate achieve goals that he has been actively involved in establishing, and later joint

[6] D. McGregor, "An Uneasy Look at Performance Appraisal," *Harvard Business Review*, May-June, 1957.

evaluation of how well the goals have been achieved, with primary emphasis on the subordinate's self-evaluation.

Some companies failed to see the fundamental difference between the two approaches. They made certain superficial changes in procedure without altering a style that was much like the first of the two described above; thus, they adapted to their own situation. New personnel forms, a new label ("management by objectives"), and new tactics were introduced, but that was all.

These companies have generally been dissatisfied with the results of their efforts. Many of them have concluded that the ideas proposed in the article were idealistic, impractical, or just plain wrong.

Experiences like this sometimes are the cause of fundamental misunderstandings between the behavioral scientist and the managerial practitioner. The latter tends to be impatient with what he considers purely theoretical and to insist on being told how to do it. His interest is in the technique, the program, the gadget, the hardware. The behavioral scientist, on the other hand, tends to be convinced that hardware is of secondary importance. Human beings are capable of substantial inventiveness along such lines. The real problem, as he sees it, rests on a change in cosmology or values followed by a modification in style. From his point of view, if these relevant causes are modified, the invention of hardware becomes a relatively simple process of inventing new *tactics*, or selecting among an array of already available alternatives. The misunderstandings thereby engendered are not at all easy to resolve.

The important point about the difference between changing tactics and changing style is that the former is usually easy, while the latter is complex and difficult. It is difficult because it is potentially threatening—or at least it is *perceived* as threatening—to the manager's basic adjustment, to his role as he conceives it. Logical argument, persuasion, managerial policy decisions, and even direct pressure are seldom effective in bringing about significant alterations in style.

Even valid scientific evidence—clear-cut, unambiguous research data—is not always effective. In fact, if such evidence is perceived as threatening, the more valid and objectively clear it is, the more threatening it becomes *if it challenges deep-rooted beliefs and convictions associated with an existing managerial style.* The "out" then is often a flat rejection of behavioral science and, necessarily, of behavioral scientists as well. Again, rational-emotional human beings can readily convince themselves of the rationality of such a reaction. Objective reality (in this case the research data) is rarely so unambiguously coercive as all that.

A few years ago I was asked by a sizable company to study employee reactions at various organizational levels to company policies and practices and in particular to general managerial style. The request came from top management, and I was given a relatively free hand with the expectation that I would bring back an objective assessment. I was assured that they really wanted to know the facts.

The method I chose was that of the group interview, in which the interaction among six or eight people at a common organizational level might be expected to yield good clues about major reactions both positive and negative. I took precautions to check the selection of the groups, to avoid leading questions that might bias the results, and to test the data that emerged from any one group against other groups.

What I found was a substantial amount of hostility toward what these groups perceived to be the basic style of top management. The reasons for the hostility were documented time after time by illustrations from everyday experience, which indicated that middle and lower management levels found it difficult, and sometimes impossible, to achieve what they believed were the goals of the organization because of highly restrictive control systems—established and administered by headquarters—that ignored local conditions and problems.

The data were remarkably similar (although of course the illustrations varied) in units that were widely separated geographically. There was a substantial flavor of frustration, discouragement, and outright cynicism about top management's managerial style—at least as these people saw it reflected in practice.

I reported my findings carefully and in detail. Certain illustrations were sufficiently common that I could report them without revealing the identity of my informants. I tried not to appear hostile (I wasn't) or to attack top management. I drew no conclusions, but simply presented the data.

The reaction of most of the group to whom I reported my findings was flatly negative. My methods were criticized on the grounds that group interviews tend to give the deviant troublemaker an opportunity to infect whole groups at a time. It was asserted that all I had collected was a series of inflated gripes and that I had missed the real feelings of the organization altogether. I was rejected as an idealistic longhair who could not perceive the facts when they were in front of his face. Along with this, for some years, went a general mistrust of behavioral scientists and their ways.

The persistent nature of the problems I had uncovered, along with the passage of time and the normal turnover in top management, has modified this initial reaction. The problems *were* part of objective reality and could not be ignored indefinitely. Some of the problems have now been successfully dealt with, and new key personalities have brought about alterations in management style.

The lesson for me in this experience was to discover how threatening facts can be when they challenge management style and management views of reality too abruptly and too sharply. I can understand better now why reports and recommendations originally requested by management so often end up gathering dust on office shelves—if they don't produce a more drastic reaction.

I have come to believe that the presentation of facts and theories, utilizing conventional intellectual methods of training and education, may often be ineffective when the subject matter involved is related to the perceptions of managers with respect to their own ideas and to the nature of man. The most fruitful methods are those which utilize direct experience of a not too threatening kind, a safe environment for the open examination of issues, opportunities to test new behaviors, and positive reinforcement of such changes as do occur. It is difficult to define what is "too threatening," in part because there are wide individual differences among managers, and some are far more easily threatened than others in this area.

PSYCHOLOGICAL DEFENSES AND MANAGERIAL STYLE

Some of the controversy over sensitivity training and the fears expressed about its potential dangers reflect exactly this problem. Methods which are so safe that they would arouse no emotional reactions would probably also be innocuous enough to produce little change. On the other hand, methods that are too threatening tend to be rejected.

My experience has not persuaded me that the threat in sensitivity training is dangerous for the manager whose psychological adjustment is within a broad normal range. The threats and pressures inherent in the day-to-day operation of most large companies (and many small ones as well) are associated with many well-known consequences such as ulcers, heart disease, and breakdowns. Because the individual in a sensitivity training program can choose to accept or reject what is "taught," he is under less threat than he well may be on his job. It is necessary, of course, to build as many safeguards into the process as possible so that individuals can reject ideas and implications that are threatening (i.e., to keep the freedom of genuine choice in the open), and to demand adequate training and professional competence among those engaging in such training activities. When these conditions are fulfilled, the dangers are rarely significant. Naturally, though, there will be individuals who are unaffected by the program, and others who will respond with outright hostility toward it.

For reasons unknown to me I find the word "style," applied as it here is to managerial behavior, unattractive. But I have been unable to find another term in common use that conveys my intent as well. One obvious choice would be "strategy," but I have not used it until now because I wish to make a distinction of some importance between the method of coping with organizational reality which evolves out of trial and error and is not deliberately adopted or even fully recognized by the individual, and which I have called his style, and a method that is deliberately planned and adopted. The latter I will call a "strategy." It has many of the same implications that it has in military usage.

Such managerial approaches as hard, soft, and firm but fair are sometimes strategic, but are more often "styles" that are given a label *after* they have evolved. The distinction, therefore, is not absolute, but relative. The *professional* manager will be defined in part by the fact that he copes with reality in terms of a strategy, although his strategy will never be completely free of influences from his original personal style. Let us now turn to managerial strategies.

5

a planned managerial strategy

A manager's style, as I have indicated above, tends to evolve from the interaction among three interdependent sets of factors: his cosmology, his identity, and the organizational situation in which he finds himself. These sets of factors are interdependent in that a change in any one has some effect on the others. His style is his typical way of coping with the situation, which in turn is strongly influenced by his cosmology and his identity.

Under ordinary circumstances this evolution is the result of trial and error rather than conscious, deliberate planning. The manager's verbal statements about his style are after-the-fact generalizations that involve considerable rationalization. Often what he says about his style appears to others to be inconsistent with his day-to-day behavior. This is why managers are sometimes surprised when a test like the Blake Managerial Grid (see Chapter 4) suggests that their style is in fact different from what they had believed it to be.

The importance of managerial style as a causal factor affecting the economic performance of the organization is well recognized today. Many programs of management development and management training include as one of their goals the development of a systematic, consciously planned managerial style based on a particular cosmology and a particular conception of the managerial identity. It will be useful to distinguish between managerial styles which are largely the outcome of trial-and-error coping and those which are deliberately and consciously elected. The latter arise out of a process of systematic planning. It is appropriate to call them *managerial strategies.*

One consciously planned and deliberately adopted managerial strategy would result from taking into account what has been discussed in the previous chapters of this volume. It would reflect the political, economic, and social characteristics of society. It would be adapted to the immediate system that it is designed to influence. For example, a managerial strategy appropriate for an industrial research unit would not be appropriate for an automotive assembly line, even though the two might have in common certain underlying beliefs about the nature of man.

The cosmology underlying a managerial strategy may be relatively (although never completely) objective. It may include descriptive scientific generalizations about the nature of human nature and about organized human effort. However, a managerial strategy is also influenced by identity. Therefore it will be *norma-*

tive: affected by value judgments. To select a strategy and plan its development, these value judgments need to be explicit. Accordingly, before outlining a managerial strategy that appears to me to be consistent with current behavioral science knowledge, I shall try to be explicit about my values. A manager whose values differed in major ways would arrive at a different strategy even though his cosmology were the same.

EFFECT OF VALUES ON CHOICE OF STRATEGY

To use Peter Drucker's felicitous phrase, "Business and industry are the economic organs of society." Their primary function is to produce wealth in the form of goods and services for human consumption. In our economic system the survival of such enterprises depends upon their ability to compete successfully in the market-place.

Successful competition in our society involves much more than the amount of wealth produced by a given firm relative to its competitors. This is why Drucker insists, rightly I believe, that the economic goal of an enterprise is not the maximization of profit but the avoidance of loss. The quest for profit is limited by a host of other considerations that society imposes on the management of an enterprise. Some of these are formal and legal: child-labor legislation, laws regulating collective bargaining, laws regulating restraint of trade, tax laws. Others are less formal social norms and standards that management must take into account in choosing the means by which it seeks profit. These change with time and circumstances, but if they are ignored by management, they tend to become formalized in what is often called restrictive legislation.

Such norms have to do, for example, with the maintenance of integrity in relations with customers, stockholders, the government, and employees. Others relate to the health of both customers and employees and to our society's norms about the basic rights of individuals. Clearly, the successful survival of an industrial organization requires attention to such values even though the profitability of the enterprise may be reduced thereby.

A norm that is currently developing in our affluent society concerns the balance between work and leisure. Leisure provides, among other things, opportunities for the satisfaction of higher-level needs. The growth of popular interest in the handicrafts, music and the theater, the arts, travel, sports, and other forms of activity all indicate that opportunities for intrinsic rewards associated with higher-level needs are becoming increasingly important. Thus a shorter workweek may one day become a social norm to which management will be obliged to conform.

One attitude toward this trend is that it is all to the good. It is the sensible answer to technological unemployment. Moreover, technological developments will make it increasingly difficult to provide opportunities for intrinsic rewards at work, not only for workers at the bottom of the organization, but for lower and even middle management as well. The answer for all but the few is to encourage the trend toward less work and more leisure, to utilize our increasing affluence in part to create more opportunities for intrinsic rewards in the rest of life, and to accept that part of life spent at work as a drudgery necessary in order to avoid deprivation of physical and security needs. Thus the rewards associated with work for most people would be purely extrinsic, and the human relations concerns of management would largely be limited to the issues of equity. Business and industry would become truly and narrowly the "economic organ of society."

The argument is persuasive. It may be that this is the direction in which we will move. It may be that my needs and values as a professional for whom a meaningful career is a central part of the satisfaction of being alive blind me to the nature of reality. Perhaps the term "leisure" carries for me unnecessary and unreal connotations of inactivity and lack of purpose and meaninglessness. Clearly human beings *are* capable of utilizing free time for constructive and meaningful (even if not economically gainful) purposes. Perhaps the "good society" will be achieved only when most of us have the time and the energy to create it.

THE VALUE OF ORGANIZED HUMAN EFFORT

What dissuades me from accepting *all* the implications of this argument is a fairly simple and to me obvious consideration: The "good society," whatever form it may take, *will be created only by organized human effort.* Perhaps some day a much smaller proportion of the population will be engaged in producing economic wealth. However, a considerable fraction of that group will certainly be professionals for whom a meaningful career in an organized system will be profoundly important. They will not settle for extrinsic rewards alone.

What of the rest of us, then, if such a society should develop? Since our basic needs would presumably be satisfied by a minimum of work in economic enterprises, conceivably we would fritter our lives away in leisure activities. This hypothesis is untenable in the light of what we know today about human nature. Man's social and ego needs would lead him inevitably into *meaningful, organized* forms of effort, not into indolence. An affluent, and by then much more highly educated, population would seek intrinsic rewards in the pursuit of new goals, in the innovative solution of new problems. New organizations, new institutions would be created for these purposes.

The problems of the management of organized human effort (in industry and elsewhere) would thus not only remain, but be intensified by the competition for talent that would no longer be attracted by the promise of extrinsic rewards *alone*.

My thesis, influenced certainly by my values, is that it is man's nature (unless he is prevented by deprivation or by poor health physically or mentally) to utilize a substantial amount of his time and energy in meaningful work associated with long-term goals. To the extent that his physical needs are reasonably satisfied, those goals will be determined by his higher-level needs. Most people will perceive the opportunities to pursue their goals in membership in such formal organizations *with whose goals they can link their own.* These organizations may be economic enterprises, noneconomic institutions (educational, governmental, etc.), or professional associations. A minority will pursue their goals independently (e.g., small business owners, novelists, playwrights, musicians). *The more affluent the society, the more significant do meaningful careers* (the pursuit of these long-term goals) *become to its members.*

THE VALUE OF MEANINGFUL WORK

I have described some "far out" possibilities. But have I? My view of reality in the United States today is that these trends are already clearly present, although only to a limited degree. Some managements today, whether intuitively or on the basis of consciously planned strategy, are attempting to cope with the changing reality. The resultant modifications of style or strategy and of tactics are most apparent within certain subsystems of their organizations (research and development is a prime example), and that is a natural response to the situational change. The important question is whether management can perceive and interpret the forces at work in our society that may require more drastic modifications of strategy within a few decades.

Meaningful work is an important part of a satisfactory life, and the degree to which work provides opportunities for intrinsic rewards is important to the total survival of an affluent society. While it may be that some types of work provide no opportunities for such rewards, the evidence from a variety of sources suggests that certain managerial strategies can provide far greater opportunities than is generally realized. I do not believe, therefore, that a mere increase in leisure time without attempts to make all forms of work significant in providing opportunities for intrinsic satisfactions is an answer which will satisfy our society for very long. The balance between work and leisure may well shift somewhat, but I believe that society will put increasing pressure on management to adopt strategies which take into account man's needs for a satisfying work career.

NEGATIVE VALUE OF MANIPULATION

Another important variable influencing my view of an appropriate managerial strategy is a negative one which concerns those forms of influence that I would describe as "manipulative." By this I mean those influences which give the illusion, but not the fact, of choice. They involve hidden motives on the part of the influencer. They are expressed sometimes in managerial circles by phrases like "Make them *feel* important" and "Give them a *sense* of participation." Open, admitted coercive influences are for me far more desirable than manipulation. Such coercive influences moreover are quite necessary at some times and under some conditions.

My reasons for being negative with respect to manipulation, thus defined, are both ethical and practical. The ethical one is obvious:

Manipulation reflects a lack of integrity. The practical reason concerns the danger of backfire if the manipulation is recognized. The resultant mistrust is likely to be long-lived and difficult to overcome. Moreover, it produces strong negative side effects. It encourages the use of ingenuity to defeat managerial purposes.

SELF-ACTUALIZATION

A final value is central to my view of an appropriate managerial strategy. It has to do with a motivational characteristic which Maslow calls *self-actualization* and which others have labeled with terms like self-realization and self-expression. This is not, perhaps, a separate human need. It is a term that describes the full utilization of human capacities to perceive, feel, learn, acquire skill, exercise intellectual capacities, create, love—in short, to grow toward the full realization of human endowments. A biological plant, under the proper environmental conditions, "actualizes" the potentialities inherent in the seed from which it sprang.

The small child, in a family climate of love and support, demonstrates the tendency toward self-actualization quite naturally. He utilizes all his developing capacities to explore and manipulate the environment, to develop skills, to create and invent. He expresses a high degree of curiosity and eagerness for knowledge. He gives and receives love. Even at the level of physiological needs, there is evidence to indicate that small children can choose an appropriate balanced diet if sufficient choices are available.

Of course, the full exercise of the child's capacities often results in interference with others. Moreover, unless he is protected, the child in the exercise of his capacities can easily be hurt or even killed. Therefore, there is a necessity for processes of socialization to curb some of his natural tendencies. But setting limits, denying impulsive infantile demands for immediate satisfaction, and restricting freedom of activity tend to be frustrating and often lead to aggression and hostility. These reactions, too, must be curbed. Even the inanimate environment can be frustrating to the child and lead to aggressive behavior.

As a result of these necessary processes of socialization, the individual tendencies toward self-actualization become overlaid by educational processes designed to make the child a responsible member of society. These processes begin in the family and extend to his relations with peers, to formal education, and to a variety of other institutional forces. The outcomes of socialization vary widely in different cultures. The behaviors that are rewarded or punished differ. The severity of punishment differs. Physical deprivation varies with the availability of necessities like food, but there is also social deprivation associated with love and support that varies from culture to culture. The cosmology and the values of each culture are reflected in its socialization processes.

Certain early deprivations and certain kinds of socialization processes produce hostility, guilt, and anxiety that may have lifelong consequences for the degree to which the individual can in fact actualize his potentialities. Our knowledge is still highly tentative in this area, but there is beginning to be clinical evidence that under proper conditions—which is to say proper modes of socialization— the child can learn to accept limits, to control his own impulses, to delay certain gratifications and deny himself others, without diminishing materially his natural tendencies to seek self-realization, to utilize to the full his capacities, to grow, and to develop.

The adult social environment, including the nature of the relationships that the individual has with meaningful "others," affects self-realization throughout life. The early family and school environment has the most profound influences, and it may limit the possibility of self-realization permanently. (People thus limited are usually termed neurotic.) The thesis I hold along with certain of my colleagues is that the reasonably normal individual remains capable of a high degree of growth and development (of self-actualization) throughout his life depending upon the social environment. Power relationships like those with parents and siblings in childhood are important parts of this environment. For the adult in a formal organization these relationships are recreated symbolically and they have high emotional significance.

Managerial strategies therefore can hinder or facilitate self-actualization. Argyris has made a persuasive case for the fact that many traditional strategies are hampering in this sense.[1] The basic point for me, however, is the firm belief that the capacity for self-actualization which is so obvious in the small child remains in the

[1] C. Argyris, *Integrating the Individual and the Organization.* New York: John Wiley & Sons, Inc., 1964.

adult even though it may be latent because of environmental restraints.

INTEGRATION AS THE CENTRAL STRATEGY

It is of course a question whether management has any legitimate concern for individual self-actualization in an organization committed to the achievement of economic goals. Some managers say no. This is the concern of the individual (or perhaps more widely of society) off the job. The requirements of organized human effort along with technological considerations clearly prevent any meaningful degree of self-actualization on the job. These needs, even if they do exist, are incompatible with the requirements of enterprise.

Some managers say yes to the question in a qualified way. A paternalistic managerial strategy is seen by such people as the way to encourage self-actualization. But a paternalistic strategy in fact involves control of extrinsic rewards. It is a matter of being good to people by giving or withholding certain kinds of benefits. It is not the creation of an environment that provides opportunities for intrinsic rewards. Therefore, a paternalistic strategy does not in my view create conditions for self-actualization.

Some people (including myself) see a genuine potential for a linkage of self-actualization with organizational goals. The possibilities are not equal for all people because some are prevented from self-actualization by the exigencies of early experiences. The possibilities are not equal on all jobs, but they are not precluded on most.

Strategy planning that takes into account this assumed human characteristic can lead *both* to a better society and to a more effective organization in sheer economic terms. It is a way of tapping latent resources of creativity, skill, and knowledge that are otherwise unavailable to the organization.

A strategy that deliberately makes self-actualization one of its goals need not involve major limitations on profitability. It may involve costs, but the expectation is that these will be more than compensated by the savings in costs which otherwise would be entailed in overcoming neutral or passive attitudes toward organizational goals. The costs of certain kinds of control procedures and incentive plans are by no means minor.

My view then, clearly influenced by my values, is that one of the fundamental characteristics of an appropriate managerial strategy is that of creating conditions which enable the individual to achieve his own goals (including those of self-actualization) *best* by directing his efforts toward organizational goals. "Appropriate" in this context means taking account of all the factors discussed in Chapters 1 and 2.

Such a strategy is *not* permissive management, or soft or indulgent management. It includes clear demands for high performance, clear limits consistently enforced. The latter are, in fact, necessary for the individual's psychological security, for him to be able to predict what is possible and what is not. It involves clear, open communications about the pressures and limits imposed by reality. It does involve the creation of a climate of genuine mutual trust, mutual support, respect for the individual and for individual differences. Only in such a climate can latent tendencies toward self-actualization find expression. Even then, the process may occur slowly and with much tentativeness at first. It is to be anticipated that some percentage of any employee group (perhaps of the order of 10 percent) will not respond at all or will take advantage of such a strategy. For such people the firm enforcement of limits, followed if necessary by dismissal, is the only feasible course. Otherwise, there is danger that indulgence toward such individuals will affect the whole organization negatively.

VALUES AND IDENTITY

The values that I have stated are part of my identity. I perceive my role as a human being and a behavioral scientist to include the promotion of them. I share them with some of my colleagues, and not with others. They certainly affect my interpretation of objective scientific evidence. I do not believe it is possible for me to eliminate their influence on my views concerning appropriate managerial strategies. Those who hold sharply different values will necessarily interpret the evidence differently and arrive at different managerial strategies.

Making allowance, then, for these values, it becomes possible to discuss a managerial strategy that is consistent with the findings of the behavioral sciences as I interpret them. This is but one strategy among many possible ones. It would apply within the context of the social, political, and economic conditions of our society today.

THEORY X AND THEORY Y

In an earlier volume I discussed certain characteristics of two rather different managerial cosmologies.[2] One, which I called Theory X, included certain beliefs about human nature that seemed to me to be rather widely held by industrial managers in our society. The other, which I called Theory Y, included some contrasting views about the nature of man that I felt were consistent with current behavioral science findings. It was not my intention to suggest more than that these were *examples* of two among many managerial cosmologies, nor to argue that the particular beliefs I listed represented the whole of either of these cosmologies.

Reaction to the publication of that book has raised a number of issues that I will attempt to clarify in later portions of this volume. One such issue is particularly relevant to this discussion of managerial cosmologies.

Theory X and Theory Y are *not* managerial strategies: They are underlying beliefs about the nature of man that *influence* managers to adopt one strategy rather than another. In fact, depending upon other characteristics of the manager's view of reality and upon the particular situation in which he finds himself, a manager who holds the beliefs that I called Theory X could adopt a considerable array of strategies, some of which would be typically called "hard" and some of which would be called "soft."

The same is true with respect to Theory Y.

I have not found it necessary during the five years since *The Human Side of Enterprise* was published to change the major assumptions that I stated there. However, today I would add to the list. Considerations such as those discussed in this chapter would yield further assumptions about the nature of man and about cause and effect in human behavior that would be consistent with the different cosmologies of Theory X and Theory Y.

Cosmologies do not lie on a continuous scale. They are qualitatively different. The belief that man is essentially like a machine

[2] D. McGregor, *The Human Side of Enterprise.* New York: McGraw-Hill Book Company, 1960.

that is set into action by the application of external forces differs in more than degree from the belief that man is an organic system whose behavior is affected not only by external forces but by intrinsic ones. Theory X and Theory Y therefore are not polar opposites; they do not lie at extremes of a scale. They are simply *different* cosmologies.

It should be apparent that one could find managerial beliefs about the nature of man sufficiently different from X or Y that they might be labeled Theory A or O or S. How many different theories there are would thus become a matter for empirical investigation and classification. I have argued only that the beliefs about the nature of man which are implicit in Theory X are part of a cosmology held by some (perhaps a large) number of managers in our society today, and that the beliefs of Theory Y are part of a different cosmology held by another (perhaps small) number of managers.

It seems to me to be far less important to categorize and label managerial cosmologies than it is to understand their development, their impact on managerial strategies, and the implications for them of behavioral science knowledge. In the present volume, therefore, I have attempted to approach the whole subject in a way which minimizes the importance of categories and labels.

part three

**IMPROVING
ORGANIZATIONAL
EFFECTIVENESS**

6

the organization of work at the worker level

A few years ago there was a flurry of interest in *job enlargement.* Several companies, including IBM, Sears Roebuck, and Detroit Edison, undertook to increase the responsibilities of certain routine jobs as a way of minimizing some of their unpleasant features. The idea of meaningful tasks rather than highly specialized, repetitive operations appeared to offer possibilities.

Job enlargement had only a small impact on industry, but it brushed the edges of some important concepts about the organization of work. A decade of study of work organization in British coal mines conducted by Eric L. Trist and a number of colleagues associated with The Tavistock Institute of Human Relations in London has produced dramatic evidence of its motivational importance.[1] Their work is destined to become a classic.

SOCIOTECHNICAL SYSTEMS

These researchers found sizable differences between two forms of social organization (sociotechnical systems) associated with a single technology under comparable circumstances. The technology was a partially mechanized longwall process of mining. One form of organization—called by them "conventional"—was the outcome of traditional industrial engineering practices. The work is subdivided into small components, and individual workers are assigned to each specialized role. The responsibility associated with each job is deliberately limited to a minimum to provide better managerial control. The worker is paid for his individual performance. Quality control is a separate function. Assignment of workers to jobs is made by the supervisor. In short, this form of organization is the familiar one based on the principles which have evolved since Taylor's work in the first quarter of this century.

The other form of organization has a long and interesting history in British mines antedating mechanized mining. Teams of miners, *self-selected* by processes that have been formalized by agreement with the union, are responsible for the total task of coal extraction, including quality control, in a given workplace. Each member of such a team acquires all the skills required for all the tasks involved. The wages are shared by the team.

[1] E. Trist, G. Higgin, H. Murray, and A. Pollock, *Organizational Choice.* London: Tavistock, 1963.

These groups select themselves, the men choosing . . . mates of the same standards in work performance as themselves. Account is taken of an individual's capacity for physical effort, his skill as a workman, the standards of performance he sets for himself, his known pattern of attendance, his age, etc. Because men of like capacity tend to work together the earnings of [these] groups tend to vary widely, even for the same work place. . . . These extremes are partly the result of differences in conditions and partly of differences in ability and stamina.[2]

These customs and rules produce a . . . group which is a highly organized and stable population. This organization and stability do not stem from the management; they arise from formalization of the customs of the working group of which the [union] lodge is the guardian.[3]

Such "composite" work groups, organized to include a three-shift cycle, exercise *internal control* "through the existence of self-regulatory mechanisms within the cycle group." This is in contrast to the *external control* (chiefly detailed wage agreements) by management made necessary by the conventional form of organization.

With the support of a self-regulating cycle-group, the [supervisor] has more scope for using his knowledge and experience . . . and the idea of his becoming an operational leader is no longer unrealistic. When men are paid only for the amounts they do of selected aspects of single tasks, they take any attempt to advise as implying that they are not up to their job and therefore not worth their money. Similarly, any request to do anything additional is regarded as exploitation unless separately rewarded. This situation deprives [supervisors] of any reasonable chance of exercising technical leadership and leads to the perpetuation and concealment of inferior work practices and to resistance to learning more apposite skills. A comprehensive agreement which commits a [composite] group to an overall task legitimates motivation to improve performance and releases ability to learn. The technical advice of the [supervisor] is sought, and the leads he offers are willingly tried out. . . . Similar demands are made on senior officials, who have the opportunity of making constructive managerial use of pressure towards greater technical effectiveness arising from the primary group itself.

Technical leadership increases in importance as mechanization proceeds. Its enhanced scope, however, was already apparent on the semi-mechanized composite faces first visited by the research team . . . where the improved quality of relations with officials was in

---

[2] *Ibid.*, pp. 33–34. (With the authors' permission.)
[3] *Ibid.*, p. 35.

striking contrast to the atmosphere prevailing in conventional settings. . . .[4]

One additional quotation is relevant concerning the nature of informal leadership in the composite team:

> In exercising internal control over the cycle, the . . . groups did not make use of specific men as group leaders to more than a minimum extent, though under conditions of higher mechanization the institution of formalized internal leadership may be required. Team captains were representatives rather than executives, and the group spread cycle responsibility equally among all members. Every man carried out whatever he was doing in such a way as to further the work of others. In the conventional system, the limit of his responsibility being the boundary of his own task, he is not constrained to do this. In the composite system, this limit being the cycle as a whole, he is induced by the nature of the . . . [system] to work in a way that furthers the general objective.[5]

While simple numbers do not reflect more than a fraction of the differences between these two forms of organization (nor the reasons for them), Table 1 gives a rough comparison of results between a conventional system and a composite system under essentially similar technical and geological conditions. Differences in *geological conditions* account for the fact that thirty-eight men were involved in the former and forty-one in the latter.

TABLE 1*

	Conventional	Composite
Total manpower (3 shifts)	38	41
Number of tasks men worked at	1.0	3.6
Different shifts worked on	2.0	2.9
Activity groups worked with	1.0	5.5
State of cycle progress at end of shift, percent		
In advance	0	22
Normal	31	73
Lagging	69	5
Productivity as percent of estimated potential of the coal face	67	95

* Constructed from data reported in E. Trist et al., *Organizational Choice.* London: Tavistock, 1963.

[4] *Ibid.,* pp. 85–86.
[5] *Ibid.,* p. 86.

A "before and after" study of a changeover from a conventional to a composite system in another mine indicated a gross improvement of 20 percent. The researchers comment:

> A reorganization, less at the mercy of chance so far as team building and allocation were concerned, would have led to a more balanced and complete development of the composite system with results substantially better than thōse obtained, however much these represented an improvement.[6]

Still another study of the progressive introduction of composite forms of organization yielded an increase in productivity of 32 percent over an eighteen-month period, although "the composite organization of these teams remained seriously incomplete" at the end of this period.

These research studies were not experiments in the formal sense. The research team did not manipulate anything. They observed and measured situations as they found them. They reported the results of what were essentially trial-and-error attempts at improvement as management gained some understanding of cause-effect with respect to the organization of work.

These attempts were fraught with many difficulties, misunderstandings, resistances. They were undertaken simultaneously with major technological changes. No one feels that perfection has been achieved. Greater understanding and experience would have made substantial differences both in the methods of introducing change and in the results achieved. Nevertheless, the results are impressive.

EMPIRICAL CONFIRMATIONS IN OTHER SITUATIONS

Ahmadabad textile mills. As a result of the knowledge gained, the Tavistock group undertook to test the generality of their findings by means of a field attempt to bring about similar changes *in an entirely different industry and in an entirely different culture.* This "action research" was carried out in the weaving sheds of a textile mill in Ahmadabad, India.[7] Despite the obstacles and unpredictable

---

[6] *Ibid.,* p. 256.
[7] A. K. Rice, *The Enterprise and Its Environment.* London: Tavistock, 1963.

difficulties involved (including a strike in the textile industry during the experiment), the results obtained were quite comparable with those observed in the coal mines of Britain.

In the textile situation, incidentally, quality was much more significant and more precisely measurable than in coal mining. With quality control in the hands of the composite work teams, improvements of the order of 30 percent were obtained.

Non-Linear Systems, Inc.   The president of a small electronics firm on the West Coast of the United States undertook a few years ago to bring about improvements in his organization by changing managerial strategy in line with a theory of organized human effort like that considered in this volume.[8] Among other things, he undertook to change his work organization at all levels toward the development of composite work teams.

At the worker level, what had been a fairly typical assembly-line operation was converted into a series of seven- or eight-man (more correctly "woman") teams who worked in separate rooms in a motel-like factory. Each team was responsible for the assembly, debugging, adjustment, inspection, and packaging of a given line of product (electronic voltmeters ranging in price to upward of $5,000). A manager whose role was essentially that of technical aid and teacher was attached to each group. The groups were not self-selected, but the control of organization, production, and quality was internal to the system. All workers were paid by salary, and base salaries were established above the going rates for comparable work in the area (to ensure equity). Although there was no incentive pay, a merit system was established that provided for substantial increments of salary, but only when substantial (i.e., easily verifiable) increases in performance occurred.

Many other changes were involved in the managerial policies and practices of the company, and we shall consider some of these later. The results attributable to changes in work organization are appropriate here.

Productivity increased over two years by about 30 percent. With

[8] *This is a reference to Andrew Kay, President of Non-Linear Systems, Inc. The interested reader may want to pursue this case study further through the writings of Kuriloff:* A. Kuriloff, "An Experiment in Management: Putting Theory Y to the Test," Personnel, November-December, 1963, pp. 8–17. *See also Maslow's recent book on his work with this company:* A. H. Maslow, Eupsychian Management, Homewood, Ill.: Richard D. Irwin, Inc., 1965. (*Eds.*)

respect to quality, customer complaints decreased by 7 percent. As of today, there are virtually no quality defects (in a highly complex and varied product assembled by hand) other than those attributable to "delayed component failures" that could not be predicted at the time of assembly.

Most of the workers are women, many of them housewives whose working supplements the family budget. On the basis of experience in industry generally, one would not expect to find a very high degree of identification with the work task and commitment to organizational goals among such employees. Their interests lie elsewhere. It is both interesting and significant to see the commitment that develops among these employees.

The groups assign workers to tasks on the basis of their skills. The newcomer is assigned simple tasks, but is given the opportunity to try new activities as rapidly as she becomes competent to do so. It takes no more than casual observation to detect the high interest that develops among most of these workers (not all, to be sure) in the rewards associated with increased skill, problem solving, and status in the group. *A substantial number of them are taking courses in electronic theory outside of working hours.* (These are housewives, remember!)

The interest of these self-regulating teams in improving their own performance is another phenomenon. "Production control" consists of a chart kept by each group of the total hours required to complete a product unit. For example, as a group begins work on a particular type of instrument, the operation may take 120 hours. The production curve tends to resemble a typical skill learning curve in psychological experiments, with increases in performance accelerating at first and then decelerating as the group productivity approaches a maximum, perhaps 80 hours. However, the group constantly uses its own and the supervisor's ingenuity to find improved methods. Thus, as the curve begins to level off, it is not unusual to find sudden increases in productivity resulting from an innovative discovery by some member or members of the group. There is a great deal of sharing of such discoveries between groups (a phenomenon almost unheard of under conventional work systems).

In addition, the groups police the performance of their own members. Management will ultimately be asked to discharge a persistent laggard who refuses to conform to group norms, although every effort will be made first by the group to help such an individual measure up.

The role of the supervisor is quite similar to that reported in the Tavistock coal-mine studies. He is an expert source of help, a technical adviser, a teacher, a troubleshooter *by demand of the group*. He does not direct, control, or discipline in the conventional sense. He does not set standards of performance or exert pressure for improvement.

Again, as in the situations reported by the Tavistock research team, the road to achievement has been rocky. Unforeseen difficulties have forced modification and changes in management's attempts to develop this strategy. External changes in the market have put severe pressures on the organization at all levels. However, the flexibility and understanding with which adjustments to environmental pressures have been made is one of the outstanding characteristics of this organizational system.

CONDITIONS FOR IMPROVING ORGANIZATIONAL EFFECTIVENESS

Here, then, are three examples of changes in organizational effectiveness associated primarily with modifications in the structure of subsystems and in methods of control. The specific methods used were adapted to the technology and to the culture—to the nature of the E and I variables in the system—but the results appear to have significance beyond the local situation. Coal mining, textile weaving, assembly of electronic instruments; Great Britain, India, the United States. It is true that one hesitates to claim universality, but certainly the argument "But our situation is different" becomes less convincing without evidence. The first case was "discovered"; the other two represent deliberate applications of theory. Let us examine a few of the more important similarities in the relationships among system variables revealed by these cases and consider their relevance to the behavioral science knowledge discussed in previous chapters.

1. The subsystem.   In each of these cases the appropriate unit of organization is considered to be *an interdependent team with a primary task*. Team size varied from seven or eight to forty-one. The combination of individual skills within the team varied widely. The primary task is different in each case.

The primary task is a meaningful whole which individual members can comprehend and with which they can identify. It is complex enough to offer opportunities for learning, improvement in status, and genuine problem solving. The group provides opportunities to achieve the many rewards which are important to "social man." The opportunity exists for the development of a cohesive team.

2. Self-control.   Each subsystem is to a high degree self-regulating. In one case its members were self-selected and in the others they were not, but in each case the groups largely determined their own form of organization and their own work assignments within the requirements established by the nature of the primary task and the technology (the "law of the situation"). They established their own production standards and their own quality control. They accepted responsibility as a group for dealing with the problems arising in production and created a flexible organization to deal with these.

3. Supervision and management strategy.   Leadership varied with the technology and the problems encountered, but the supervisory role in each case shifted markedly from one of direction, surveillance, and control to one of providing technical help, support, and instruction. (It is interesting to note that this same shift in managerial role occurred under the conditions created in the relay test group at Hawthorne more than thirty years ago, but its significance was only casually noted.)

The typical role conflicts of supervision in conventional systems are resolved in this form of organization. The supervisor is not pulled and hauled between the role pressures generated by his superiors, staff groups (like engineering and quality control), and his own subordinates (whom he is expected to befriend, lead, help, and control at the same time).

The *transactional* character of influence has been recognized, accepted, and built into the management strategy.[9] The members of

---

[9] *"Transactional"* is a term that McGregor found increasingly congenial to describe a mutuality and collaboration between the leaders and the led and situations in which influence expands rather than "equalizes." (Eds.)

the work groups have a much greater degree of control over their own fate than under conventional strategies. Intrinsic rewards of high importance are involved in this change. On the management side, experience under such circumstances contributes to a more realistic appreciation of the potentialities of "average man," to a reduced fear of the power of groups, and to a marked reduction in bureaucratic controls, fulfilling the requirements of which occupies (nonproductively) a major part of the time of the conventional supervisor.

4. Motivation. In addition to the motivational characteristics noted above, the reasons for protective and defensive behavior on the part of the work team, and for the utilization of skill and ingenuity in beating the system, are removed. Conditions have been created such that the members of the work system can achieve their own goals to a much greater degree by directing their efforts toward organizational goals.

One of the highly interesting consequences of the composite system in the British coal-mine study concerned absenteeism.[10] Here are the data:

TABLE 2   ABSENCE RATES (PERCENT OF POSSIBLE SHIFTS)

Reason	Conventional	Composite
None given	4.3	0.4
Sickness and other	8.9	4.6
Accident	6.8	3.2
Total	20.0	8.2

No managerial control, no safety program produced these results. *They were correlates of the form of work organization.* While the causes are not definitely known, it seems probable that in the composite system the improvement is the result of increased psychological security in a dangerous environment. Under the conventional system, each man (or two- or three-man group) is on his own, expecting neither to give nor to receive help from others when he is in trouble. Under the composite system, the team effort includes a considerable amount of mutual support. An analysis by the re-

[10] E. L. Trist and K. W. Bamforth. "Some Social and Psychological Consequences of the Longwall Method of Coal-getting," *Human Relations*, vol. 4, pp. 1–38, 1951.

searchers of absenteeism accompanying increased strain produced by technical difficulties supports this interpretation of the data.

Here, then, is an excellent example of an important increase in organizational effectiveness realized through changes in the organization of work rather than by the exercise of any of the conventional forms of power. It illustrates the difference between mechanical and organic conceptions of motivation. A better safety record (by more than 100 percent) was achieved not by control of external rewards or punishments, but as a by-product of *removing restraints* created by organization structure and thus *permitting* existing motivation (security needs) to influence behavior. The issue of the relative value of hard, soft, or firm-but-fair managerial strategies is completely irrelevant to this change in organized human effort.

Some criticisms. Critics—both in the behavioral sciences and in management—have raised a number of issues with respect to the broader implications of the theory underlying cases such as those discussed above. One of the major ones is an opinion—based primarily on evidence from conventional organizational systems and partly on convictions concerning the nature of man—that most people are dependent, don't want to accept responsibility, prefer to be led, and prefer to seek higher-level need satisfaction *off the job.*

About the only response to this criticism that seems to be appropriate is: "Maybe so, but take a look at this evidence." The implications from these examples are not that the behavior and attitudes displayed by these employees are universal, or that similar changes could be made in every organization. But the evidence does suggest that some managements in some organizations might find it worthwhile enough to test. The inference we can draw challenges some basic aspects of conventional theory.

A second issue is whether results like these are a mere replication of what is referred to today as the *Hawthorne effect.* The results obtained at Hawthorne were not maintained over time. It has been argued that the novelty of the situation, the great interest shown by higher management in the experiment (manifested by frequent visits to the site), and the status that accompanied the unique treatment of these workers were the real causes of the changed performance. When these causes were removed, or when their effects wore off (the argument goes), performance reverted to "normal."

Interesting to me is the fact that these particular causes are cited but the changes in the organization of work and in managerial control are ignored. The relay test groups at Hawthorne were put back into the conventional organization structure and under conventional supervision. It was *then* that performance reverted to normal! It is a nice question as to which causes were necessary and which were significant. In the coal-mine study, *none* of the causes attributed by the critics to the Hawthorne effect were present. In the Indian textile study, the results were maintained over several years until there were major changes in management strategy. (The company has so far not permitted a study of these changes and their effects.) In Non-Linear Systems the changed conditions have been maintained for four years at this writing with no indication of a Hawthorne effect. On the contrary, the organization has successfully weathered a fairly severe crisis brought on by shifting market conditions.

It seems reasonable to conclude that this issue concerns an interpretation of cause and effect. In the cases we have considered, *and at Hawthorne,* the results were maintained as long as the conditions (the system changes on which they were based) continued.

The only other major criticism which seems to me to merit attention here is that the behavioral science theory underlying these and many other current attempts at improving organizational effectiveness puts major emphasis on *power equalization.*[11] This, some critics feel, either is not a good thing or is unrealistic. Like myself, Argyris, Likert, Haire, and a number of other behavioral scientists have been criticized along these lines.

If the point is that we have interpreted behavioral science knowledge to indicate that transactional forms of influence are more effective than unilateral ones, I, at least, plead guilty. The cases cited above, and other evidence to be cited later, all involve a shift in the balance of power—*in particular* in the recognition of the consequences of abuse of legitimate authority and coercive controls. I find the evidence substantial for the assertion that unilateral power is *in fact* a fiction, except possibly under the most extreme conditions of physical coercion.

These conceptions, however, do not imply power *equalization.*

[11] H. J. Leavitt (ed.), *The Social Science of Organizations.* Englewood Cliffs, N.J.: Prentice-Hall, Inc., 1963.

Moreover, as noted above with respect to the coal-mine absenteeism data, it is important whether "power" means the traditional mechanical "force on passive human object" form of influence or whether it means the kinds of influences that produce improved performance in an organic system. With respect to the latter the power has not been equalized; it has increased *for management and workers alike.*

HOW TO DO IT

The difference between a limited tactical change like job enlargement and a major strategic change like that involved in these cases should by now be evident. It is easy to see how the former can be accomplished without change in managerial cosmology or strategy. Not so the latter.

Their differences highlight the problems created by management eagerness for easily applied "patent-medicine" cures. While much could be learned by seeing what others have done in any of these cases, the visitor would not return with a package or a formula to be installed with minor "adaptations to our circumstances." More than lip service to the principles of the tailor-made improvement would be required.

The formula for how to do it involves first obtaining enough acceptance of behavioral science knowledge with respect to the nature of man and of organized human effort to create a willingness to undertake the costs and the risks of the necessary development. Then a detailed mutual study, such as that undertaken by A. K. Rice at Ahmadabad, needs to be made of the present work organization and of possible modifications that would yield appropriate sociotechnical systems. Finally, a pilot-plant experiment would need to be made to test the value of the plan evolved from the study, to "iron out the bugs," and to obtain the kind of data that will provide the basis for deciding whether to extend the plan into normal operation.

Such a process might easily take three to five years and require considerable risk capital in manpower, time, and money. In addition, it would require a substantial amount of ingenuity and inventiveness, and a willingness to place the pilot plant "under an umbrella" to protect it from conventional organization pressures until an adequate test can be made. Such pressures include not only those connected with control systems, but the normal movement of managerial personnel through promotion and transfer and the impatience of higher management for "results."

These conditions are fulfilled to a greater or lesser extent in product or process research and development. Somehow, management usually finds it difficult to see the analogy to research and development in the field of organized human effort. Without this commitment to the development of human assets, and without a clear understanding that providing for the growth of human resources is a painstaking and difficult task—but ultimately worth the effort—management must resort to recipes, fads, and other "instant cures."

In this chapter I have attempted to state some principles about improving organizational effectiveness from the annals of research in strikingly different settings. These principles, if they can be called that, emerge from an elaboration of the assumptions of Theory Y. The major elements are (1) an interdependent team, (2) self-control, (3) the transactional character of influence, and (4) intrinsic motivation. In the following chapter I try to take account of some newer developments which I have had a hand in (and which occur at the managerial level). Some of the principles stated here will be tested against my own consulting experience.

7

the organization of managerial work

Unpublished internal company studies in several industries during recent years reveal similar experience with respect to the voluntary turnover of "college hires." During the first five years of employment the figure is of the order of 50 percent. Moreover, there are indications that many of the better rather than the poorer people are among those who leave. Some follow-up studies indicate also that one of the major reasons is that "the job didn't utilize what I've got to offer" in the form of training and capability.

The cynic will reply that the underlying cause of these phenomena is the unreasonable, unrealistic perception of the college graduate of his own ability. There is some truth in this assertion, but in my judgment not much. There is also truth in the argument that company recruiting practices tend to *create* such expectations by making, or at least implying, promises of opportunities that are unrealistic. Follow-up studies by my colleague Edgar Schein of a sample of our graduates at the master's level for several years after graduation tend to substantiate the latter argument.[1]

THE MAIN DISTORTION: UNREALIZED POTENTIAL

I become steadily more persuaded that perhaps the greatest disparity between objective reality and managerial perceptions of it is an underestimation of the potentialities of human beings for contributions to organizational effectiveness. These potentialities are not merely for increased expenditure of effort on limited jobs (although such potentialities do exist) but for the exercise of ingenuity, creativity in problem solving, acceptance of responsibility, leadership in the relational sense, and development of knowledge, skill, and judgment. When opportunities are provided under appropriate conditions, managers are regularly astonished to discover how much more people contribute than they had believed possible.

My years as President of Antioch College reinforced this view considerably. To observe under the cooperative plan the highly responsible positions in which some employers placed our students,

---

[1] E. H. Schein, "How to Break in the College Graduate," *Harvard Business Review,* November-December, 1964, pp. 68–76. See also E. H. Schein, *Organizational Psychology.* Englewood Cliffs, N.J.: Prentice-Hall, Inc., 1965, chap. 3.

and to hear the consistently high praise from these employers—not for a single student, but for a series of them who had followed each other for the short period of three or four months—was a bit startling, even with my high initial expectations. To discover in the administration of every phase of the college activities how responsibly and effectively students took their places alongside faculty members under Antioch's community government system was equally fascinating.

When friends visited the college, I enjoyed inviting them to observe meetings of the Administrative Council, composed of elected students and faculty and chaired by me; the Council was the equivalent of the executive committee in many industrial organizations. The Council determined educational policy; established the budget, which was then submitted to the Board of Trustees for final approval (and rarely altered by the Board!); selected faculty; and made most of the college's major policy decisions. My suggestion to my visiting friends often was: "Pretend you cannot see what is going on. Tell me afterward if you could have guessed which members of the Council were students and which were faculty." The answer almost every time was: "Not possibly." (Remember, the students were undergraduates.)

My general point is that surprisingly often organizational management in industry, education, and elsewhere determines its strategy and organizes work on the basis of a major underestimation of the potential capabilities of its human assets. The findings with respect to the turnover of college hires are but one reflection of this rather consistent misperception. Some of the reasons for this phenomenon have been alluded to in earlier chapters. However, my interpretation of the evidence leads me to the conclusion that a major opportunity for improved organizational effectiveness lies in a reconsideration of the *organization of work* of employees at every level up to the top.

Let us consider the situation at the level of the exempt salaried employee (managers, staff specialists in all functions, engineers, scientists, and the like).

A motivational study, by Frederick Herzberg and colleagues, of engineers and accountants in a sample of manufacturing firms in the Midwest revealed that in addition to the intrinsic rewards associated with work that permitted full use of the individual's talents (as he perceived them), a reasonable degree of autonomy and opportunities for personal growth were among the primary concomitants of high morale and high performance.[2] On the other hand, working conditions, company benefits, supervision, and even salary to a major degree were not nearly as potent motivators for these employees. In fact, they were sources of *dissatisfaction and low performance unless they were equitably administrated.*

This study dealt with individuals. Other studies (for example, the work of Donald Pelz[3] with scientists and engineers in research laboratories) have not only resulted in similar findings but have added weight to the findings reported in Chapter 2 about socio-technical systems at higher organizational levels. The systems at these levels are organized around intellectual rather than physical technologies, but the basic evidence appears to be similar for both. One of Pelz's findings from a series of studies is that the most productive research scientists are found in situations where the processes of determining work objectives are transactional rather than unilateral in either direction (i.e., where both the scientist and management determine objectives). What Pelz calls the "deadly condition" for these men is the one in which standards and objectives are imposed by management alone, without influence by or collaboration with the scientist.[4]

A CASE STUDY OF TRANSACTIONAL ORGANIZATIONAL CHANGE[5]

The president of a company in a major public utility system became concerned a few years ago about two problems related to the structural organization of his company. It was highly functional up to the sixth level of management. As a result, he believed, men

[2] F. Herzberg, B. Mausner, and B. Snyderman, *The Motivation to Work*. New York: John Wiley & Sons, Inc., 1959.
[3] D. C. Pelz and F. M. Andrews, "Autonomy, Coordination, and Stimulation in Relation to Scientific Achievement," *Behavioral Science*, vol. 11, no. 2, pp. 89–97, March, 1966; and D. C. Pelz and F. M. Andrews, "Organizational Atmosphere, Motivation and Research Contribution," *American Behavioral Scientist*, vol. 6, pp. 43–47, 1962.
[4] D. C. Pelz, "Freedom in Research," *International Science and Technology*, vol. 26, pp. 54–66, 1964.
[5] *For a more detailed account of this case, since published, see K. LeCompte, "Organizational Structures in Transition," in Mason Haire (ed.), Organization Theory in Industrial Practice. New York: John Wiley & Sons, Inc., 1962.* (Eds.)

in certain key positions did not develop *general* managerial skills early enough in their careers (although they were rotated to some extent among the specialized functions). In addition, he felt that this organizational structure promoted narrow departmental loyalties rather than concern for the business as a whole. It appeared to him also that friction rather than cooperation was thus generated in too great a degree between functional departments. In addition, the business was facing increasing mechanization and technological change in the next few years.

The vice-president of personnel, who had taken a leading role in working with the president and other officers of the company on long-range organizational problems, then established a one-man organizational planning staff in the personnel department. He appointed a manager with wide experience in the business and gave him broad latitude to look at other organizations and to seek professional help, as necessary, in an effort to reach a solution to these problems. The president has since said that he expected to be presented, perhaps in six to eight months, with a new organization chart, the major change probably being a lowering of the level at which a *general* manager was placed.

The new staff man chose to look around not only at other companies but at behavioral scientists working in the field of organization. He obtained the services of one of them as a "strategy consultant," and together they discussed the relevant findings in the field. They then conducted a series of interviews with a sample of middle and upper-middle managers to discover how these men felt about the president's concerns and to learn whether there were other associated problems that should be considered in planning the major reorganization. They found concurrence with the president. In addition, they found general perception of problems relating to the organization of staff functions and their relationships to the line management, problems connected with the level at which various decisions were made (it was often felt to be too high), and many others.

After considerable discussion, both of behavioral science theory and of the situation in the company, the planning staff, with the full support of the vice-president of personnel, presented a proposal to the president and his cabinet. The strategy for change involved utilizing the know-how of members of management in analyzing the existing system by means of a multilevel task force chaired by a top-level executive. This group, in turn, would seek help in the form of factual or analytic studies and recommendations wherever they needed it within management. They would attempt to formulate a set of recommendations for a reorganized structure which would meet the objectives of the program and which would take into account the original concerns of the president, the related problems that had been revealed by interviews with middle management, and any relevant new problems uncovered by their work as a task force.

It was further suggested that the planning for change be public, not secret, and that full information on the work and plans of the task force would be made available to all managers to the extent possible. Their reactions and suggestions would be encouraged. (Note the transactional character of the whole strategy.)

Finally it was suggested to the president that if the recommendations of the task force were acceptable to him and to his top management, a "pilot trial" be established to test the new form of organization for at least two years. Both before and during the experimental period, the management of the new unit would be encouraged to help improve the plan in ways indicated by their experience.

The crucial moment came when the two organization planners indicated to the president that their suggestions would probably take five years to implement fully, although the task-force and pilot-trial phases might be completed within two years. He was first shocked, then incredulous, but he listened to the rationale. Finally he agreed, once he understood that things would not stand still for five years, but that partial implementation would occur as fast as practicable. "I'd like to see something significant accomplished before I retire," was his comment.

The task force was created. The organization planners became consultants to it. About nine months of study was involved. The final report contained recommendations for a number of structural changes. Certain functions were centralized, others decentralized; and a considerably altered form of relationship between staff and line was proposed. For our purposes here, the major recommendation was the formation of a *team* of fourth-level general (not functional) managers in each of the geographic subdivisions of the organization, headed by a fifth-level general operations manager. Thus the role of general manager was placed two levels below its place in the existing structure. The proposed concept of the managerial team was in major respects comparable with the "composite" form of organization in the coal-mine studies, adapted, of course, to the managerial levels which were of concern here.

For the pilot phase, it was suggested that a new geographic subdivision be created by splitting an existing one that had become too large. The new managerial team would be given several months to study the proposed plan, *organize themselves* as a team, and plan the implementation. The pilot operation would function for about two years (while continuous data would be obtained about its operation) before consideration would be given to extending it. Meanwhile, it was expected that during the initial phases—perhaps for several months—the performance of the new organizational unit would be substandard. There were many specific problems to be solved, changes to be made in work assignments at lower levels, changed relationships to be developed with the rest of the company groups, new policies and practices to be installed. It was suggested, therefore, that top management "hold an umbrella" over the pilot unit until the new organization solved its initial problem and settled down. This might take the better part of a year. Then a few months of relatively stable operation would provide more normal data on the performance of the new organization.

With respect to performance, the report of the task force noted that the purposes of the reorganization did not include improvement in the day-to-day sense over the performance of the existing organization. Therefore, performance (including costs) comparable with that of existing organizational units should be acceptable, although the task force confidently anticipated measurable improvement. The major goals, however, were improved service to the customer, improved management development, minimized functional loyalty at the expense of the business as a whole, and reduced interfunctional friction.

The proposals of the task force were accepted with minor revisions, and the new managers of the pilot unit were appointed and went to work to plan their take-over several months later. The organization planners worked with the new group, attempting particularly to help on matters of team development, internal relationships, and the processes of objective setting.

Certain environmental pressures necessitated the speedup of this planning phase, and the new team began operation somewhat hastily a couple of months ahead of the originally scheduled date. In addition, and somewhat unfortunately, the new unit became involved almost immediately in an independent but major series of changes connected with the installation of new computerized accounting procedures. Nevertheless, there was high enthusiasm among the team members, and they tackled the rather massive array of problems facing them with the confidence typical of a pioneering group.

RESULTS OF THE PROGRAM

One major phase of the reorganization plan turned out to be impossible to realize. This concerned modifications in company-wide control systems. It had been hoped originally that these modifications (similar in conception to those characteristic of the cases discussed in the previous chapter) might be given an adequate trial in the pilot operation. However, the "umbrella" collapsed under fairly massive environmental pressures. The team maintained internal control over their organizational structure and in certain other respects, but this collateral objective feature of the original plan had to be abandoned.

An intensive interview study was conducted toward the end of the eighteen-month pilot operation. Members of the new team, their immediate subordinates, a sample of lower-level supervisors, and a sample of management clear to the top of the organization were queried in depth about their reactions to the new form of organization. The results were generally positive.

The members of the team were enthusiastic. Even the limited degree of greater autonomy they had gained was highly rewarding. The rewards—extrinsic and intrinsic—associated with team membership and team operation were perceived to be substantial. Almost without exception they stated that they were working harder than at any previous time in their careers with the company, *but enjoying it*. A number of troublesome problems associated with the traditional form of organization either had been or were in the process of being solved. There was no question but that they felt their own development as managers was enriched and accelerated under the new organization. Many decisions were being made at lower levels, and more appropriately. Their concern for the business as a whole had become dominant rather than secondary. The staff-line relationships had improved greatly.

Except for some members of lower supervision who felt that their managerial problems had remained unaffected by the change, the rest of the new unit seemed to be genuinely positive about it. Managers in the larger system had encountered a few difficulties in adjusting to the changed relationships brought about by the change, but they too were in general quite positive.

After consideration of these and other data, top management decided to extend the new form of organization to the remaining areas of the company, involving an additional twenty-two thousand people. However, there was clear agreement that this should be accomplished area by area, giving several months for planning and development to each successive managerial team. The transactional character of the operation was continued. An area task force composed of the top management of the area and other specialists was set up and proceeded to study the experience of the pilot unit and to consider whether modifications were needed in adopting the plan in their unit. The broad increase in internal team control contemplated by the task force plan was eliminated.

Today, *some six years* after the original task force was established, the reorganization has been completed in all four areas of the company. *There has been virtually no resistance to this very substantial organization change.* In fact, there has been rather general impatience in each successive unit with the delay until they could get going.

In spite of the initial agreement that comparable performance under the old and the new structure was acceptable, the evidence is conclusive that *improved* performance has resulted with respect to most of the performance measures used by this company. It is impossible to measure in any precise or direct way the degree to which the original objectives of the president have been achieved, but anecdotal evidence and the perceptions of team members and top management alike suggest that these objectives are being achieved. One can only speculate about whether the achievement in all respects might be greater if it had been possible to maintain the degree of internal team control contemplated by the original model. It is evident from informal discussion that many members of the new team think so.

TEAM BUILDING AT UNION CARBIDE CORPORATION

In 1959 a member of the headquarters personnel staff in a large manufacturing company attended a seminar sponsored by the Foundation for Research on Human Behavior and devoted to organization theory as it was developing out of behavioral science research. Although he began as a skeptic, he became convinced of the soundness of the theory and returned home determined to test it in practice.[6] A little later he was made head of a small unit called "organization development," which, in addition to the functions implied by the name, was responsible for the headquarters staff aspects of exempt salary administration and management training and development. The unit reported to a corporate vice-president of industrial relations.

With his then six (now eight) subordinates, he then undertook to apply the theory to which he had become committed. The initial objective was to develop a composite sociotechnical system that would itself be a pilot test of a new form of organization. This was a self-development project to which all the members of the team quickly became committed. Because the function was new, there were few precedents, and top management was quite willing to permit experimentation.

Team development did not proceed in an ivory tower. The group had work to do: providing staff help to top management and to a considerable number of divisions on all phases of organization planning, developing an improved salary administration plan, providing assistance and advice on training and development. Accordingly, they attempted to build their own organization around their major tasks—the "technology." This involved them in a number of critical issues associated with their methods of providing staff help to line management as well as their own internal organization and their relations to each other. The twofold purposes of team development and performance of their tasks proceeded simultaneously, and with the central underlying purpose of applying behavioral science knowledge and theory to both. As the process went on, they read and discussed some of the relevant literature and occasionally

---

[6] *There is no need for anonymity now since* Fortune *(November, 1965) has publicized Union Carbide's organizational development and the author's influence on the "skeptic," John Paul Jones. (Eds.)*

brought in some of the authors for further discussion and consultation on their problems.

Early in their existence much time was devoted to a meaningful statement of their role in the company, their purposes and objectives (short and long range), and the principles by which they proposed to guide their behavior. The process was transactional in a number of ways. First, it was a genuine process of *group* planning in which all the members, including the manager, participated. Second, as they clarified their views, they discussed them with the vice-president to whom the unit reported. The initiative for these discussions came from them, not from him. Third, when their formulations became fairly well developed, they circulated them to all the officers and major department heads in the corporate organization, asking for reactions and expressing willingness to discuss any points of disagreement.

Their initial document contained the following statement of their overall objective:

> To assist in developing and implementing better principles of organization, motivation and management with respect to the efforts of administrative, technical and professional people.

This was followed by a statement of policies:

> 1. The aim of an Organization Development consultant is primarily to provide insight, perceptions and principles to assist the manager or his organization in developing for themselves the kinds of solutions which best meet the problems at hand.
> 2. The services of a consultant are available upon request. He will not seek to interject such services where they are not wanted.
> 3. An invitation to consult, advise or assist on any specific or given problem does not commit the seeking manager or organization to any continuing relationship with the Department or consultant, nor does it commit him to accept counsel nor the principles on which counsel is given. Similarly, consultants expect to be free to withdraw from situations where they feel they cannot be helpful.
> 4. In formal conceptual work, the Department expects to be held fully accountable for the integrity of the principles evolved. On the other hand, once a formal system, procedure, or program has been adopted by line management, the accountability for its operation belongs with the line.
> 5. Time and availability permitting, any member of the Department will accept an invitation from any manager to work with him and

his organization on their problems and will report findings only to that manager and his organization unless specifically asked by that manager to convey data to his organizational superiors.

6. The members of the Department will not misuse confidential information entrusted to them by either formal or informal means, but within the Organization Development Department such information is not confidential. Free and complete internal exchange of data and experience is necessary to maximize learning and competence. (The essence of this policy is an attitude of mutual trust, mutual support and open communications which allows for complete exchange of ideas, experiences and problems among members of the group as needed. The sharing of every conversation and problem is not an internal objective of Organization Development, but like partners in any effective consulting organization we are often compelled by the needs of the client to consult among ourselves to try to produce the most useful help for the client.)

Finally they stated in some detail the specific goals which they had established for the following year. Samples of these goals are:

Under certain conditions, the Department will assume the initiative for feedback on the operation of administrative systems to those responsible for initiating or directing them. Such feedback will be initiated only when:

a. The operation of the systems appears to be creating problems within the organization.

b. The feedback will not violate a confidential relationship between members of the Organization Development Department and other persons.

c. The decision to feed back will not violate a specific consulting relationship between this Department and other organizations within UCC.

Organization Development does not assume that the offering of such feedback entitles the Department to further involvement in the problem or its solution.

Each year since, they have followed a similar process, including a statement about the accomplishment of each previously established goal. The basic statement of purpose has been modified as a result of the group's perception that the "environment" has changed, and with it the company's needs in relation to their function.

This process of formulating the group's primary task and associated goals takes a lot of time each year. Nevertheless, the resulting identification with the task and genuine understanding of all its subtle implications are a major influence on their day-to-day behavior. From their point of view the time spent is not only worth it; they believe firmly that they could not operate as an effective team without going through the discussion and sharing of experience involved in this kind of joint planning.

The chart of their organizational unit, incidentally, consists of a *circle* of photographs that includes each member of the group, the manager of the unit, and the vice-president to whom the unit reports. Lines from each photo connect to a central box within which there is a statement of their primary task. As they perceive it, the members of the unit, including their boss, report to an objective rather than to a person. That objective is the result of a transactional process in which the whole corporate management surrounding the unit has had an opportunity to become involved. Moreover, it is steadily influenced by reactions of their "clients" throughout the company.

In the period since the unit was formed they have provided internal consultant help—*on request*—to subsystems within the company from bottom to top and within several major divisions. The projects on which they have been consulted have ranged from limited problems to reorganizations extending over months.

A major project of the latter kind began in 1963 and at the time of writing has continued about eighteen months. One member of the organization development team has been more or less continuously involved in the project with the help of other members at various times.[7] At one point the whole team assisted in an intensive interviewing project to provide the particular management with data on certain problems. The internal problems of this client organization have been thoroughly explored by its management (which has developed into a fairly strong composite group during the process), and a variety of changes in policy and in organization structure are now being implemented. The lower levels of the organization have been actively involved in this analysis and planning. The major existing problems are those between the field organization and headquarters top management, and the member

[7] *This refers to George H. Murray, Jr., who is now John Paul Jones's successor as General Manager of Organization Development of Union Carbide Corporation.* (Eds.)

of the organization development unit is now working jointly with these two groups to resolve some of these problems.

Utilizing similar transactional processes, a new plan of exempt salary administration has been developed, discussed, and accepted and is now being implemented—on request of individual divisions as they wish help—throughout the company. This plan is most unusual in the degree to which it is based explicitly on behavioral science theory. The document that describes the plan includes a detailed statement of its theoretical rationale. (The rationale was presented by a member of the team recently to an audience of professional salary administrators. The response was one of high interest and rather general concurrence.)

Similarly, a carefully worked-out plan for obtaining *voluntarily* detailed information about the experience, training, and career interests of exempt personnel throughout the company is being implemented currently. The data are being stored in a computer program so that all potential candidates for an opening can be located. One underlying purpose of the plan is to make it possible for employees to have an active role in their own career development rather than to remain passively receptive to the whims of fate.

These are but a very few examples of the work of a small unit which is beginning to have significant impact on management strategy in a very large organization. The overall effect seems much like a process of "infection" with what I, as a behavioral scientist, conceive to be a benign disease.

The internal operation of this team is remarkably effective today, although there is constant attention by the members to the improvement of their methods of operation, their individual skills and knowledge, and their performance. It would not be easy to find a staff unit in the headquarters of any of the large companies with which I am familiar in which there is greater commitment to the task or more enthusiasm in accomplishing it. Moreover, the relationships of this group with line management throughout the company are remarkably constructive. There is virtually none of the suspicion and antagonism on the part of the "field" that is so commonly found toward headquarters staff. On the contrary, the requests for help are growing at a rate that raises questions about the team's appropriate size and the possibility of developing internal consultants like themselves within divisions.

SUMMARY

In the last two chapters I have tried to exemplify the conditions that enter into improving organizational effectiveness through a transactional process of change based on research findings and direct experience. The general theoretical considerations concerning the value of composite sociotechnical systems are strengthened by what has happened and is happening in the situations described above.

part four

**POWER
AND CONTROL**

8

the administration of managerial controls

THE NATURE OF CONTROL SYSTEMS

The information feedback control loop is a process by which information about past or present performance is used to influence future performance. Its engineering applications to machines and processes are so common and so well understood today that extended discussion of them is unnecessary.

In a managerial control system the same principle may be applied to human performance—to budgets, to cost and quality control, to the profit center, to incentive plans, to performance appraisals, and to many other organizational activities. The applications range from naïve to sophisticated; the measures of performance may be simple ratings or judgments, or they may be highly intricate and precise statistical sampling methods. All, however, stem from the same basic principle.

The information feedback control loop is an essential, universal aspect of human behavior. Information from the outer world and from inside our bodies is transmitted via feedback loops in the nervous system, enabling us to guide virtually all our conscious actions and triggering many unconscious ones. Knowledge of present or past behavior is essential for any change, for learning, for improved performance.

There is a fundamental difference between the engineering and the human applications of the principle of the information feedback control loop. Machines and physical processes are "docile"; they are passive with respect to the information fed to them. They can respond, but only to the extent that the alternative forms of response have been designed into the machine or the process. (Recent developments in the simulation of mental processes by the computer indicate that these statements may require qualification. They can stand, however, for our purposes here.)

A more fundamental distinction is that emotions aren't involved in the feedback process with machines or technological systems. This distinction, often ignored, is critical. As it becomes conceivable that the computer may one day be able to perform a great variety of human intellectual processes, and that it may do so at a rate many orders of magnitude faster than that of the human brain, some intricate and fascinating issues arise about the place of man in the world of the future.

With few exceptions, the discussion of these issues ignores the interdependence between man's intellectual processes and his motivational and emotional ones. This same phenomenon occurs characteristically in the planning and administration of managerial control systems.

A human being's perception of information about his own performance involves selection and either acceptance or rejection in varying degrees. The process of responding to the feedback of information involves both intellectual and emotional reactions that are largely inseparable. As a result, the human being exercises self-control in his responses. Management's expectations (usually borne out in practice) is that the response of others to information feedback about performance will tend to range from a low degree of compliance, through indifference, to some degree of noncompliance. (Compliance and noncompliance are variables in both intensity and spread.)

To compensate for these expectations—to counterbalance the likelihood of noncompliance—management introduces administrative procedures into the information feedback loop. These consist in standards of acceptable performance, in objectives, in extrinsic rewards for compliance and punishments for noncompliance.

UNINTENDED CONSEQUENCES OF CONTROL SYSTEMS

The introduction of administrative procedures into the feedback loop represents a major modification of the fundamental engineering principle. It is necessary, but it results in complications that are widely experienced but not at all well understood.

There will be a fair degree of agreement, in my belief, with the statement that such procedures work, but rather less well than managers desire. They do yield compliance to some degree. But in addition they yield:

1. Widespread antagonism to the controls and to those who administer them.
2. Successful resistance and noncompliance. This occurs not with respect to a few people but with respect to many. It occurs not alone at the bottom of the organization, but at all levels up to the top (and sometimes there also).

3. Unreliable performance information because of (1) and (2) above.
4. The necessity for close surveillance. This results in a dilution of delegation that is expensive of managerial time as well as having other consequences.
5. High administrative costs.

Actually, most of these consequences are fairly readily observable inside any large organization. To different degrees they are characteristic of virtually all managerial control systems. Finally, these undesired consequences are rarely eliminated by the tactics usually adopted to improve the administration of control systems.

There are exceptions to the generalizations outlined above. Some of them are rather dramatic. In a few organizations, the administration of managerial control systems leads to quite different consequences:

1. The systems work significantly better than the usual ones. There is substantially more positive *self-control* exercised over performance.
2. Antagonism toward the controls and toward those who administer them is low or absent.
3. Resistance is essentially absent.
4. The performance data provided by the system are reliable—they are a true reflection of performance.
5. There is high delegation and little surveillance.
6. The administrative costs are low.

These organizations have made deliberate use of existing behavioral science knowledge in designing and administrating information feedback control systems. In particular, this approach is consistent with two reasonably well-established generalizations about human behavior in organizational settings. These generalizations are not simple, they are not precise, but they can be translated into practice.

REACTION TO THREAT

Noncompliance tends to appear in the presence of perceived threat. This noncompliance takes the form of defensive, protective, resistant, aggressive behavior. Note that I have used the words "perceived threat." Feelings are facts! The question is not whether management believes that the control procedures are threatening; the question is whether those affected by them feel that they are.

There are several conditions under which threat is likely to be perceived. One is where punishment—as opposed to support and help in meeting standards and objectives—is emphasized. Where the feeling is generated that the employee must conform "or else," the sense of threat is common. The data cited by Rensis Likert from the many studies conducted by the Institute for Social Research at the University of Michigan consistently indicate that pressure of this kind for higher performance is rather generally perceived to be threatening.[1] The evidence of noncompliance comes from the units where pressure of this kind is steadily used as part of the manager's strategy. Performance tends to be lower than in units where such pressure is minimal or absent.

A second condition in which threat is likely to be perceived is where trust is lacking in the relationships involved. These relationships include both those between superior and subordinates and those between the line and the staff people who administer control programs.

A third condition arises when the feedback of information negatively affects the individual's self-esteem, his career expectations, his emotional security in the employment relationship. The study referred to earlier of the effects of a conventional performance appraisal program clearly revealed the presence of threat under these conditions.[2] The evidence of its presence was the observed defensiveness of the subordinate.

How management induces threat.   Let us consider some features of conventional management control systems that may create threat. First, pressure for compliance with externally imposed standards is a common tactic. It is clear with respect, for example, to accounting controls, budgets, the performance standards of the boss, industrial

[1] R. Likert, *New Patterns of Management.* New York: McGraw-Hill Book Company, 1961.
[2] E. Kay, H. H. Meyer, and J. R. P. French, Jr., "Effects of Threat in a Performance Appraisal Interview," *Journal of Applied Psychology,* vol. 49, no. 5, pp. 311–317, 1965; and H. H. Meyer, E. Kay, and J. R. P. French, Jr., "Split Roles in Performance Appraisal," *Harvard Business Review,* January-February, 1965, pp. 123–129.

engineering standards of work, and the like. In one large organization, those responsible for an elaborate system of performance measurement are explicit in their philosophy. It is: "Measure everything you possibly can, and use the measures as needles." In this organization, it is firmly believed that performance could not possibly be as high as it is without this strategy of control. All the side effects mentioned above are readily to be observed at middle and lower levels, but the attitude at top management appears to be that these costs are probably inevitable, and not very important.

If noncompliance continues or reappears under this kind of pressure, the reaction is to increase the pressure. In one company top management acquired incontrovertible evidence that many of the performance measures on which they relied were in fact unreliable because the data were "fudged" in one way or another. The evidence suggested that this phenomenon existed not only at lower levels, but well up into middle management.

The response of top management was to create a committee of high-level executives to explore and examine these phenomena and their causes and to make recommendations for correcting the situation. After substantial study (in which they were assisted by the staff group who designed and administered the control systems!) they made three recommendations:

1. Eliminate as far as possible any collection of information in which the individual is responsible for reporting his own performance or any aspect of it.
2. Initiate a series of audits (some of which were audits of already existing audits).
3. Announce to the organization in unmistakable terms that anyone involved in manipulating the data would be promptly fired.

If, as seems highly probable, the behavior which this company sought to correct was caused by pressure that induced threat, it is interesting to speculate whether increasing the strength of the cause would correct the behavior. Yet this is a very common tactic, although it is often less obvious than in the case cited. Many cost reduction programs operate in this fashion; so do management's attempts to deal with restriction of output under incentive plans.

Another device, common to many managerial control systems, that is likely to induce threat is represented by the concept of "accountability." The logic of accountability within the framework of conventional managerial principles is clear. However, it takes relatively little experience with or observation of the operation of this principle in everyday organizational life to recognize that its practical use is to discover and punish noncompliance with externally imposed standards and controls. The real meaning in practice of the principle of accountability is: "Find out who goofed."

Control through measures of "variance" operates similarly to emphasize mistakes, failures, and substandard performance.

Staff attitudes and staff affiliations are another substantial source of threat. Staff groups often display an attitude of mistrust toward those who are affected by the control systems that the staff have designed and are administering. One can argue whether the source of such mistrust lies in an unconscious selection process through which people with long-standing mistrust of their fellows gravitate into such positions, or whether it lies in staff experience with typical responses to conventional control systems. Regardless of whether the chicken or the egg came first, it is readily observable that staff groups who administer control systems have a fairly low regard for the honesty of those affected by them.

Another aspect of staff involvement in the administration of controls has to do with the natural affiliations of staff groups. Typically, the manager of a staff organization reports to a line manager a level above him organizationally. Quite naturally, his conception of his role is to assist his boss, to behave in such a way as to obtain approval from the boss. In the performance of his role it is unlikely, to say the least, that he will consider it a major responsibility to support and help line managers at his level and below about whose performance he is collecting information for his boss to use. Almost regardless of the policies that may be stated about the relationship of staff to line, the conventional organization structure and mode of operation generates these attitudes. It requires a different system structure and a different set of relationships to generate trust and support between the line and those staff groups who administer information feedback control loops.

Finally, consider the normal flow of information in the feedback loop. The information may flow back to the individual whose performance is being "controlled." Almost universally, however, it flows back also to the level above him, and sometimes to several higher levels. Moreover, it may flow to those higher levels in specific detail.

Sometimes it goes to higher levels before it goes to him, and sometimes it goes to higher levels without going to him at all except as his boss sees fit to feed it to him.

Without arguing the logic or the necessity for these channels of information flow, I would state it as a simple fact that when such information is critical of a man's performance (when it reveals mistakes or substandard performance of the individual or of those below him in the organization), *threat is involved.* Moreover, the threat is substantial because it may carry implications for his long-run career in the organization.

The principle of management by exception, under which only variances from standard are fed back to high levels, *could* be a positive motivational device if the emphasis were on recognition and reward for variances *above* standard. I have yet to encounter an organization, however, in which the principle is utilized in this manner. "Control" in practice means discovering, correcting, and punishing negative variations from standards.

Let us carry the analysis one step further. If the above generalizations are sound, it would seem probable that one could successfully predict at least some forms of noncompliance which would be evidence of the presence of threat:

1. The first prediction would be of simple failure to comply with demands for change when perceived threat exists. A former Sloan Fellow at M.I.T. conducted a rather simple but revealing research project to test this prediction relative to one type of managerial control—performance appraisal. In the company that he studied, there was a standard and well-administered performance appraisal program. The general manager was strongly in favor of performance appraisal, and he had supported it openly and approved of the training of his subordinates in administering the program and conducting appraisal interviews.

Reasonably good records were made and kept centrally. Thus it was possible to go through the records over a period of time and select all the cases in which a superior had requested a change in the behavior or performance of a subordinate during an appraisal interview. The subordinates and superiors in question were then interviewed to find out whether (a) they both remembered the request for change, and (b) they agreed that the change had occurred. He found agreement that it had occurred in approximately 10 percent of the cases! This study, coupled with that described above which demonstrated the correlation between defensiveness and criticism in an appraisal interview, makes a fairly strong case for the prediction.

2. Another prediction would be that in the presence of perceived threat human ingenuity will be exercised to defeat the purposes of the control system. William Foote Whyte's *Money and Motivation*[3] presents ample evidence, in a series of case studies, of the high degree of ingenuity which the average human being can display under such circumstances. In fact, the general recognition of this phenomenon under all types of control systems is sufficient to persuade many managers that a foolproof control system would be impossibly costly if it could be devised.

The real cost, however, of such behavior is the diversion of human creativity in this direction. If half the human ingenuity now exercised in this way could be tapped to increase organizational effectiveness, the gains would be startling.

3. A third predictable form of noncompliance in the presence of threat is dishonesty. Moreover, one could further predict that the perception of threat would become a justification and a rationalization for the dishonest behavior. Melville Dalton's *Men Who Manage*[4] provides some convincing documentation at *middle levels of management* for these two predictions.

There is a common and mistaken tendency to attribute a dishonest act by an individual to a characteristic of his personality. Thus implicitly we divide the population into two categories: dishonest people and honest people. There are individuals who display dishonesty consistently in a wide variety of situations. Such a characteristic almost always reflects mental illness—a form of personal adjustment that lies quite outside the normal range. (There are also people who are so compulsively honest, even in the most trivial matters, that they may be said to represent a form of maladjustment also.) A dishonest act by the average man, however, tends to be specific to certain circumstances and is not the manifestation of a general character trait. It is in this sense that we can say quite truthfully: "Most people tend to be fundamentally honest."

Certain sets of circumstances, coupled with certain cultural norms and standards, will produce behavior that is dishonest in varying degrees on the part of many people who would, in most other

---

[3] New York: Harper & Row, Publishers, Incorporated, 1955.
[4] New York: John Wiley & Sons, Inc., 1959.

aspects of life, be scrupulously honest. Automobile traffic regulations and the Federal income tax are obvious examples. So are a great many managerial control systems. The error is to seek the cause in the dishonesty of human beings rather than in the pressures to which they were subjected. Just as individuals try to "beat the system," organizations try to "beat the rascals."

A president of a chain-store concern told me recently of an experience along these lines. In seeking to reward good performance and to motivate higher performance among his store managers, he had installed an ingenious bonus system involving sales and costs of operation. After it had been in use for some months, he came into the possession of evidence that certain of his managers had found ways of manipulating the system so that they could get bonuses which were not reliable reflections of their actual performance. He called his managers together and told them that *he had made a mistake.* He then informed them in full detail, without naming names, what he had discovered. He concluded by saying: "I would like to provide a financial bonus that truly represents above-average performance by store managers. Can you help me devise one that will not tempt you into dishonest practices? I cannot feel that I am treating you fairly if we have any practice or policy that tempts you in this way." A group of his store managers, after some work, presented a plan which everyone agreed minimized the temptation to manipulation. I suspect personally that their reaction to his way of handling the situation was a powerful force affecting their behavior under the revised plan. In any event, he was satisfied that the problem was solved. In my experience with managerial control systems, this is a real example of man bites dog!

4. One other prediction concerning noncompliance in the presence of threat is based on the fact that human beings (unlike machines or technical processes) can distinguish between the numbers used to measure a performance and the performance itself. This human ability can and does become the basis for an exciting game known as "getting the numbers." Almost everybody likes to play it, not only because it requires the exercise of ingenuity and involves risk, but because it provides a very satisfactory outlet for hostility. When they perceive threat, people tend to react with hostility. Since it can be directed not only toward the organization as such, but toward the people who design and administer control systems, the issue of the dishonesty involved becomes neatly buried in the excitement of the game.

The generalization that emerges is that conventional managerial control systems have a strong tendency to generate and accentuate the very behavior they seek to prevent: noncompliance. The reason, fundamentally, is that pressure for compliance in a climate lacking in mutual trust and support leads to the perception of threat. The reaction to threat is hostile, defensive, protective behavior. Attempts to correct control systems designed on the basis of conventional strategy by increasing the accuracy of measurement, by audits, or by tighter controls serve simply to increase the threat. The consequences, as demonstrated above, are quite predictable.

Unfortunately the *absence* of threat does not guarantee compliance. It may lead merely to indifference, to a reduction in active noncompliance. The absence of perceived threat in managerial control systems is therefore a necessary but not a sufficient requirement for positive compliance. Let us consider, then, a second generalization about human behavior with respect to information feedback loops.

THE SENSE OF COMMITMENT

Human response to information about performance varies with commitment to goals. The purpose of any information feedback control loop is to achieve some standard of performance. Occasionally, the standard, at least as stated, is perfection. With respect to safety, the goal is no lost-time accidents; with certain clerical functions, the quality standard is no mistakes. Sometimes the goal is not perfection, as in the case of voluntary turnover where the desired standard is usually to keep below some upper limit. With respect to variables like quality of product or level of output, standards are often expressed in terms of an acceptable level. Finally, the standard may simply be improvement over present performance, as is frequently the case with sales and sometimes with cost controls.

Actual performance under any control system is significantly affected by who sets the standards and at what level they are set. Experience demonstrates that if they are too high, they will not be perceived as possible and relatively little effort will be expended in achieving them. On the other hand, if they are too low, the real potential will not be achieved. However, the reaction will be directly determined not by the objective standard, but by how it is perceived. The perception is influenced by feelings, needs, and attitudes. The significant question is: What will be perceived to be reasonable? The establishment of standards of performance by industrial engineering methods offers many examples in support of this assertion.

A mechanical cosmology underlies the administration of many managerial control systems. Management will determine what is possible and what is reasonable or necessary, often making extensive use of professional help in the process. Then the attempt is made to achieve the desired level of performance by using "legitimate" authority and extrinsic rewards and punishments. This general strategy may be qualified in many ways. For example, the process of expense budgeting usually involves the submission of proposed budgets from the various units, which are then modified at higher levels until they are acceptable to those levels.

Such a process is subject to all the side effects discussed above. What is ultimately achieved, therefore, is the result of a trial-and-error process of coping with the consequences of the standard setting. If the standards are accepted—if they are perceived to be reasonable—the results will tend to be satisfactory. If they are not, the tactics adopted will be (1) to persuade or coerce lower levels into accepting the standards, (2) to attempt to get performance within the established standards by pressure (the threat of punishment) while accepting the negative side effects or attempting to eliminate them by increased pressure, or (3) to lower the standards or accept substandard performance.

This process, based as it is upon a mechanical conception of cause and effect, tends inevitably in practice to place strong emphasis on the threat of punishment. Except in the case of incentive plans, the extrinsic rewards for compliance tend to be long range and relatively uncertain. The manager who succeeds in meeting the standards that have been set for him can hope for long-term rewards in the form of salary increases and promotion. But the probability of punishment or of the withholding of rewards for noncompliance is much more certain. Since the basic purpose is to obtain compliance with goals and standards set by others, the individual's chief motivation is to escape punishment.

Intrinsic rewards are largely ignored under these circumstances. Surveillance displaces autonomy, mistrust undermines self-regard, absence of support and help minimizes achievement, likelihood of punishment for noncompliance reduces risk-taking and innovation, rigidity of standards and administrative procedures precludes the individual's use of his own know-how. The whole process accentuates passive compliance rather than creative problem solving.

THE VALUE OF COMMITMENT

Perhaps the most fundamental difference between passive compliance and a problem-solving approach is in attitude toward the capabilities of the organization. It is not assumed that these are measurable in terms of specifics like industrial engineering standards, estimates of possible cost reduction, quantity in manpower requirement estimates, etc. Such measurements may be useful, but they don't take account of the capacity of the organization for invention and innovation. They ignore the implication of the adage that "it is not how hard but how smart you work."

In fact, from this point of view the capability of the organization is *unmeasurable*. The basic managerial strategy is to develop an organization capable of meeting external demands and pressures in such a manner that it will compete successfully. The belief is that if members of the organization are identified with this goal, they can cope with reality even when such coping involves belt tightening, force reduction, limitations in extrinsic rewards.

In order to cope with reality, the organization must know what reality is. This requires open communication, mutual trust, mutual support, and the management of conflict by working it through. The basic requirement is not mere acceptance of goals and standards, but commitment. Such commitment is necessary not only with respect to the overall successful competition of the organization but with respect to all the specific subgoals associated with performance.

The principle is that human beings will direct their effort, exercise self-control and responsibility, use their creativity in the service of goals to which they are committed. The managerial task is to help the organization achieve and maintain high commitment, and heavy reliance is therefore placed on the intrinsic power of identification. The assumption is that commitment is related to performance roughly in the manner indicated in Figure 3.

Identification and commitment rest on linking the individual's own goals with those of the organization. There is therefore heavy reliance on intrinsic rewards and punishments and on the achievement of equity with respect to extrinsic rewards and punishments.

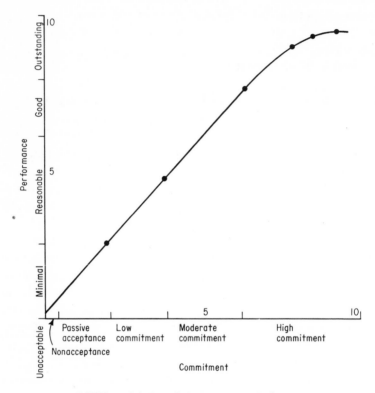

FIGURE 3. Relation of Commitment to Performance.

Donald Pelz, as a result of studies in eleven research and development organizations, comes to a conclusion that expresses the point rather well: "The autonomous scientist does not necessarily perform better than the man whose technical goals are determined by others as well as by himself. The most productive man is one with substantial control over his own goals, but who allows those goals to be influenced by others. The deadly condition is one in which goals are set by the boss alone."[5] Although this conclusion, as we mentioned in Chapter 7, relates to scientists and engineers, it is not restricted to them.

[5] D. C. Pelz, "Freedom in Research," *International Science and Technology,* vol. 26, pp. 54–66, 1964.

A managerial strategy for inducing commitment.   The strategy under discussion is based on the assumption that it may be possible to get acceptance, but it is not possible to get commitment by imposing goals and standards on others. Therefore, tactics for the establishment of standards are ones that involve the joint, open exploration of reality. Given the existence of a reasonable degree of mutual trust and mutual support, the following tactics would be consistent with such strategy:

1. An open presentation and discussion of management views of the requirements for successful competition at any given point in time. This would include an analysis of the external forces and of the internal problems reflected in the information on past performance. The latter would include an examination of possible "restraining forces" preventing a realization of the organization's capability.
2. A broad analysis of changes in performance of the organization that would be required to meet the demands of external reality.
3. An analysis by each subunit of the contribution it can make to the total organizational effort. This analysis would be conducted at each level of the organization from the face-to-face subunits at the bottom through departmental and divisional units to the top.
4. A statement from each unit of the goals and standards to which the unit could commit itself relative to (1) and (2) above. Included in the statement would be an analysis of what help the unit would need in accomplishing these goals. Such an analysis might involve certain kinds of information feedback, staff help, changes in policy or procedure, equipment and manpower needs, etc.

These tactics may appear to be cumbersome and time-consuming. However, they are based on the well-supported conviction that time spent in obtaining identification and commitment to standards and goals initially will be more than compensated by time saved in later implementation and problem solving. Except for times of crisis when major adjustments will be required, the process will take little more time than is typically utilized by other strategies.

Naturally there will be difficulties, disagreements, and conflict in this process. Management will not be passive or permissive with respect to these, however. It will exercise active leadership, and where the working-through process does not resolve the conflicts, it will invoke legitimate authority to whatever degree is necessary to establish definite standards and firm limits. The process of capital budgeting, for example, is one in which top management will play a strong role for reasons that will be obvious to all. Here the expectation would be that management will impose limits and make allocations after considering requests from lower levels.

AN ORGANIC APPROACH TO CONTROL SYSTEMS

The administration of managerial controls within a context such as this will be quite different from the conventional one. If commitment to standards and objectives has been achieved, the primary requirement becomes that of providing help to the subsystems as they seek to meet the jointly agreed goals. Each subsystem will require regular feedback and information about its performance to enable it to correct or change its operation. The task of staff units will be to provide information to each level of the organization about its performance in a form which can be used for this purpose.

There may be intersystem problems to be solved, and management of larger systems will need to provide help in their solution.

There will be periodic upward reporting from each subsystem to the next larger one. This will take the place of the usual staff reporting to higher levels. Such reports would include (1) data from the subsystem that tell the next higher level: "Here is where we are at this point in time"; (2) a statement of problems being encountered and of plans for solving them; (3) if help is needed, a specification of its nature and a request for it.

Surveillance, in the usual sense, becomes largely unnecessary under such circumstances because the problem is not one of obtaining passive compliance but of enabling all parts of the organization to achieve the goals to which they are committed. Each unit down to the individual level has a degree of control over its own fate. The total process, from the initial exploration of reality to the solution of problems arising in the day-to-day attempt to meet goals and standards, provides ample opportunity for intrinsic rewards and for the motivational effects of intrinsic punishments arising from mistakes and failures.

Naturally the development of such strategy is an evolutionary process. It would be foolhardy to attempt to shift from a conventional strategy to this one quickly or to involve all managerial control systems at once. Small-scale pilot experiments within subsystems of an appropriate size are likely to be a more effective way of testing such a strategy. Of course, in a small organization the approach can be company-wide.

(I am referring to this type of control system as *organic*, as contrasted to *mechanical*. An organic control system itself is a social invention developed out of an analysis of a particular situation, which itself evolves out of the needs of individuals and subsystems affected by the data and gathered and transmitted to the relevant systems under conditions of trust and openness.)

The research on performance appraisal in one of the units of the General Electric Company provides an illustration of this process. As indicated in Chapter 1, research on this managerial control system substantiated certain theoretical predictions concerning the threat involved in the administration of performance appraisals and the consequence of side effects.[6] As a result of these findings, a test of a different strategy has been undertaken on a pilot basis. The alternative strategy is essentially similar to that described above in that it is based on organic conceptions of cause and effect. The tactics are called *work planning*, and they are undertaken by a given manager with individual subordinates. Joint planning is undertaken periodically in the attempt to establish standards and goals for a prescribed period. Emphasis is placed on open communications, mutual trust and support, and the desirability of commitment. The information feedback loop is to the subordinate, and he in turn discusses with his superior where he stands and seeks help as needed in accomplishing the jointly agreed objectives.

In this case a careful test is being made of results by adopting the new strategy with one group of managers while maintaining the original and more conventional one with another comparable group of managers. Thus, the differences can be compared and modifications made as necessary in the new strategy before consideration is given to a wider use of it.

The modification of managerial control systems instituted by Andrew Kay at Non-Linear Systems, Inc., is an illustration of a deliberately planned strategy based on an organic cosmology in a small company. The tactics and results have been discussed in Chapter 6.

[6] Kay, Meyer, and French, *op. cit.;* and Meyer, Kay, and French, *op. cit.*

Sometimes the intuitive style of a manager leads him to adopt such a strategy in a crisis situation and thus to bring about a major change in a relatively short space of time. Such an example is reported by Robert Guest in an automobile assembly plant.[7] This plant had been consistently the lowest of six comparable plants in the measures typically applied to performance within the company. The manager of the plant had resorted to pressure in order to improve the situation. His strategy was a typical mechanical one that emphasized extrinsic punishment. The situation went from bad to worse, and higher management eventually replaced the manager with another man.

The new manager was given freedom by higher management to approach the problem in his own way. His intuitive managerial style led him to begin by attempting to remove the pressure from the organization. In an open manner he communicated to the organization his view of reality and of the necessity for drastic change in order to achieve a successful competitive level. He indicated his trust and confidence, and his desire to be supportive, by asking for help. At all levels he asked for an analysis of problems and restraining forces and offered full managerial support in solving them.

It took four years, but at the end of that time this plant was at the top of the six plants in terms of the measures utilized rather than at the bottom.

One final example occurred a few years ago in a large oil company where top management recognized that a variety of external economic forces bearing on the organization required very substantial increases in organizational efficiency if the organization's competitive position were to be maintained. The president of this company had been working for some time consistently with his intuitive style along lines which had built a fair degree of mutual trust and support in the organization. In the face of this crisis, he undertook first to communicate to the whole organization as openly as possible his view of the reality. He said specifically that he did not wish to impose specific standards or to use pressure to improve performance. Instead, he asked each unit of the organization to examine carefully its own performance and to adopt whatever procedures seemed appropriate to achieve improvement. He indi-

[7] R. Guest, *Organizational Change.* Homewood, Ill.: Irwin-Dorsey, 1962.

cated that the improvement would need to be substantial, but he did not set a figure on it.

In addition, he promised top management's support in every conceivable way. One specific tactic was to ask each of his key executives to go to a major subsystem and offer help and support. However, in order to ensure as much autonomy as possible in the analysis and planning within the subsystems, each executive was asked to go to a subsystem whose tasks and responsibilities lay outside his own responsibility and competence. Thus the executive would be less likely to attempt to impose his own analysis and prescription on the organizational unit that he visited.

A variety of other tactics were utilized, and at the end of a year the president was able to report to his organization that its accomplishments were more than satisfactory.

It is interesting to note that another oil company facing essentially the same pressures elected to follow a more conventional strategy that included the imposition of certain specific standards of manpower and cost reduction on all units of the organization. At the end of the year this company had achieved only about half of the improvement that was specified by the original goals.

The point should be clear, but it deserves reiteration that the tactics utilized for the administration of managerial control systems of all kinds are not themselves critical. Where successful results have been achieved, they can be traced to a *strategy* or an *intuitive managerial style* that in turn has been materially determined by the underlying cosmology of the management concerned. Such tactics are virtually certain not to be successful when they are "adapted" to a sharply different strategy based on a different cosmology. This would be particularly true where the cosmologies involved include a mechanical conception of cause and effect in human behavior in one case and an organic conception in the other. In each of the illustrations above, the tactics adopted were largely inventions based on the analysis of a particular situation in the light of a particular planned strategy or intuitive managerial style.

9

managerial power

A persistent problem underlying the implications of behavioral science findings with respect to organized human effort is the nature of managerial power. Management is responsible, after all, for achieving the economic goal of the enterprise, yet the traditional uses of power by management in fulfilling its responsibilities are sometimes inappropriate. Does this mean that management must abdicate, or become soft or permissive? Not at all. The implication from behavioral science knowledge is that management should become *selective* in its exercise of power. We began by noting that behavior —in this case organized human effort—is a complex function of certain characteristics of human nature, of certain characteristics of the environment, and of the relationship between them:

$$B = f(I_{a,b,c,d}\ldots E_{m,n,o,p}\ldots)$$

It has been suggested that the task of management is to create relationships among these variables such that the members of the organization perceive that they can achieve their own goals best by directing their efforts toward the goals of the enterprise. The desired result is an organizational system capable of coping successfully with the complex, rapidly changing external environment. The purpose of managerial power is to achieve this result.

If one accepts a "mechanical" conception of cause-effect in human behavior—if one believes man to be *by nature* indifferent or negative toward organizational goals—the alternatives with respect to managerial power are limited. Man can only be coerced, by threat or bribery, into expending energy in the desired direction. The possible managerial strategies are hard, soft, firm but fair, period.

An organic conception of cause-effect, on the other hand, opens a variety of possibilities for the exercise of power. If man is *by nature* motivated to expend energy in attempting to satisfy his needs (physical, security, social, and egoistic), he will select among available opportunities those which he perceives to be the best for achieving his goals. This theory assumes that the relative importance of these goals is not fixed, but varies in certain ways with the degree to which they are being achieved (i.e., with relationships between *I* and *E* variables).

The most appropriate managerial strategy, according to this theory, is to create an organizational environment in which man perceives the most attractive opportunities for achieving his dominant goals to lie in expending effort toward *organizational* goals. There are similarities between such a strategy and the marketing strategy that management uses in creating and keeping customers for the organization's products or services. Moreover, such a strategy is widely utilized today in the requirement of college graduates and technical specialists. Ordinarily, however, this strategy is abandoned precisely at the moment when the recruit becomes an employee.

A corollary of the organic theory is that indifference or hostility toward organizational goals is usually a *symptom*, rather than a cause. The cause is not the absence of motivation; it is the fact that the organizational environment is not perceived to offer the best opportunities for achieving the goals that are dominant.

It would, of course, be unrealistic to assume that management could ever create the ideal environment implied by this theory, even if cost were not a consideration. Some essential characteristics of the organizational environment in any industry (the assembly line in an automobile plant is but one example) severely limit the opportunities for the pursuit of *some* human goals. Coercive forms of managerial power are necessary under such conditions. (They are not *sufficient*, however.)

Likewise certain individual characteristics (*I* variables), under certain conditions, set limits on the forms of managerial power that are appropriate. To take an extreme case, the goals, the attitudes, the expectations of the average man in an agricultural society involved in the early stages of industrialization are such that it would be folly to attempt to influence him by methods that would be appropriate for research scientists in our society.

Although perfection may not be achievable, management has by no means fully exploited the different forms of power available. Nor have the *limitations* of traditional forms of power been recognized. While I have followed common usage in speaking of "power" throughout this chapter, "influence" is perhaps a more accurate term. The everyday implications of power as a controlling variable apply more meaningfully to extreme forms of coercion. Some forms of power consist in influence brought to bear *directly* on people. Others consist in influence exercised *indirectly* through modification of the organizational environment (organization structure, managerial controls, etc.). Let us consider what they are, and some of the conditions that determine their appropriateness and their limits.

LEGITIMATE AUTHORITY

One form of power is basic in formal organizations of every kind. The sociologists and political scientists call it *legitimate authority*. Its successful use depends on social attitudes and norms that place the right to govern or control in "offices" within social institutions. The power of kings, presidents, prime ministers, judges, and policemen is thus based. So are certain powers of the occupants of administrative or managerial offices in every organization. The social attitudes and norms involved are summed up in the concept of "consent of the governed" (even though "consent" may sometimes be obtained by coercive means). This form of power is exercised by establishing policies, procedures, and rules, as well as by making everyday decisions and giving orders.

LEGITIMATE AUTHORITY IS RELATIVE, NOT ABSOLUTE

Social norms differ from society to society and from institution to institution within societies. The power of a priest differs from the power of a manager because the norms that set the limits of legitimate power in the church differ from those in industry. The legitimate authority of a manager to discharge an employee is more restricted in a unionized plant than in a nonunionized one. The legitimate authority of a judge is different from that of a policeman. In industry, the arguments over the scope of "management rights" are usually arguments about legitimate authority.

What management perceives to be "restrictive" legislation is frequently the result of the failure to recognize the relationships between social norms and legitimate authority. Attempts to maintain absolute rights, rather than awareness of changing norms accompanied by judicious voluntary adjustments to them, are the cause of much legislation of this kind. The history of labor legislation from child labor laws to the present is the history of changing social norms with respect to the legitimacy of certain forms of power that were resisted or ignored until they were enforced by law.

This pattern is not restricted to management or to industry. It has been repeated with respect to religious institutions, unions, professional organizations, and even governments. On the other hand, many professional societies have developed codes of ethics and self-policing functions and in this manner have escaped some, although by no means all, of the restrictive consequences of public legislation.

It is possible that the trend toward the professionalization of management will bring with it similar organized forms of adjustment to social norms. In the absence of a genuine managerial professional organization today there is no forum for discussion and no organization for action with respect to such matters. Neither the National Association of Manufacturers nor the American Management Association, for example, fulfills the requirements of a professional society. The former has been essentially a lobby,[1] and the latter is primarily an educational society.

In the past, public legislation in this field has been focused primarily on the relationships between management and workers. It is not impossible that relationships within management, and between management and employees who are professional specialists, will become a matter of public concern some day.

In our society we deplore the idea that man should become the "servant of the state." This is one of the major differences, we say, between the West and the iron-curtain countries. However, in many respects today, the exempt salaried personnel in large companies come close to being servants of the corporation. Certainly practices are not designed to produce this result. Nevertheless, managerial expectations with respect to geographical movement of such personnel, the administration of promotion policies, the "career authority" exercised by managers over their subordinates, various kinds of surveillance involved in control systems, the notions concerning responsibility and accountability which take for granted that the job will assume priority over all other aspects of life including the family—these and other types of influence within the enterprise *can* create a condition that has some of the characteristics of servitude. The situation is not materially altered by the fact that many managers become willing servants rather than face "deportation." This condition is not permanent, and there are indications today that it is changing. Books like William H. Whyte's *The*

---

[1] *The NAM has, of late, moved significantly away from this narrow image.* (*Eds.*)

Organization Man[2] and Vance Packard's *The Pyramid Climbers*[3]
have had more than a minor impact.

There may be adequate *logical* justification for all the policies
and practices that contribute to this state of affairs. That, however,
would not prevent the exercise of restrictive governmental power if
the public should one day begin to perceive these practices to be
contrary to our society's values—if the exercise of authority in these
ways should come to be perceived as illegitimate.

The refusal to adopt right-to-work laws in most states provides an
obverse example. Such laws are strongly supported by many managers
and have often been initiated through their efforts. It seems probable
that the general public does not today perceive such legislation to be
consistent with existing social norms. Managerial attempts to change the
norms have so far been unsuccessful in most instances. Union leadership,
in this case, has in general stayed within the limits of the public norms
of legitimacy, but there is no guarantee that these norms will remain
what they are today.

The norms that define the legitimacy of authority are not alone
broad social ones, although these define the outer limits. Within
every organization there develops a set of norms that in some
respects is unique. These norms are a function of the relationships
between E and I variables as these have developed over time in
each organizational system. Thus we find willing acceptance of
forms of authority in one company that may be the source of active
resistance in another.

Legitimate authority in industry is neither a God-given nor a
logical right. It is a powerful form of influence so long as it is
perceived to be legitimate by those affected. The prime implication
for management from behavioral science findings about the exercise
of this form of influence is that the "consent of the governed" is
more than a pious phrase. The governed *do* set the limits, even
though they may do so only informally by resistance and by ingenious kinds of sabotage. When the norms concerning legitimacy
become explicit and general, the limits are established by formal
legislation unless management can either alter them or adjust to
them voluntarily. As we have already noted, *every* form of influence is to some degree transactional. The exercise of authority is
no exception.

[2] New York: Simon and Schuster, Inc., 1956.
[3] New York: McGraw-Hill Book Company, 1962.

CONTROL OF EXTRINSIC REWARDS AND PUNISHMENTS

A second form of power is exercised by the direct control of extrinsic rewards and punishments, among which money is primary. As already pointed out, in an affluent society—and particularly among those whose mobility is high—money becomes less a potent means for exercising power than under other circumstances. However, this does not imply that money becomes unimportant. Two things tend to happen: (1) The issue of equity becomes more important, and (2) larger increments of money are generally required in order to make effective use of this form of power.

Among top executives especially, a further limitation of the power of money to influence behavior is imposed by income tax laws. Other extrinsic rewards (many of which involve dollar costs for the organization) are in part substituted as "motivators." These include stock option plans, personalized office decoration, travel, insurance, winter vacations, and many other perquisites. An important point, however, about fringe benefits generally, in contrast to salary and wages, is that they cannot be used so directly to exercise power. They may create goodwill, they may prevent dissatisfaction, but they are less potent than salary for the exercise of power through extrinsic rewards.

Another important way of using this form of power is through the administration of promotions. Advancement in the organization brings with it not only more money, but increased status. It *may* also bring greater autonomy and opportunities for personal learning and development. It is noteworthy that these last two rewards are intrinsic and are not correlated with promotion as such, but with organization structure, managerial control systems, and amount of delegation.

Power through control of extrinsic rewards and punishments is related to power through legitimate authority. The two, however, are not identical. With respect to the latter, acceptance of employment in an organization implies a "social contract" to abide by the policies and rules of management. The great majority of employees demonstrate by their behavior that they accept this obligation. When a union is involved, the terms of the contract are made explicit through collective bargaining, and again most union members respect the contract. Authority exercised within its terms is perceived to be legitimate.

It is not primarily the threat of extrinsic punishment (demotion, suspension, discharge) or the promise of particular extrinsic rewards that brings about compliance with legitimate authority. Even though it is unexpressed, there is a genuine acceptance of a moral obligation. (This is the same attitude that leads most citizens to be generally law-abiding.) *So long as management does not violate the norms of legitimacy,* the great majority of members of the organization at all levels will comply with the exercise of power in this form.

If legitimate authority is not perceived to be exploitative or arbitrary, if it is consistent, it provides order and predictability for the members of the organization. It sets limits to be sure, but if these are perceived to be just and reasonable, and if they are firmly enforced, they too provide order and predictability: "Stay within the limits and you can count on fair treatment." When the employment relationship is perceived by the employee to have that meaning realistically, many of his emotional security needs in the relationship are met.[4]

Note that while the exercise of legitimate authority can minimize behavior opposed to organizational goals, it does not maximize enthusiastic support of them. It is a form of power that, properly exercised, creates compliance. For the manager who seeks to realize a larger contribution from his employees, it is a necessary but not a sufficient cause.

Power exercised through the control of extrinsic rewards and punishments, on the other hand, can achieve more than compliance, chiefly through emphasis on rewards. The limits inherent in the motivational value of such rewards have been discussed above. These limits do not in any sense render them useless. They do raise questions about the appropriateness of *primary* reliance on extrinsic rewards as the means of obtaining the greatest possible contribution to organizational goals in a relatively affluent society.

Perhaps the greatest difficulty associated with this form of power is the achievement of equity. It has already been emphasized that equity is determined not by those who administer extrinsic rewards

[4] *Rensis Likert pointed out to us that even under the best of conditions legitimate authority may be reacted to by some subordinates as threatening, even when they see the manager's behavior as the exercise of legitimate authority. (Personal correspondence to the editors, 1966.) Undoubtedly, with certain employees and under certain conditions this is true; but it is also probably symptomatic of underlying organizational problems. (Eds.)*

but by those who receive them. The *perception* of equity on the part of employees is the crucial factor. Equity does not mean equality. If these rewards are associated with performance (which is the only sense in which they can have motivational significance to management), their administration must lead to the perception of a genuine and consistent relationship.

Most managerial salary administration programs are thoroughly confusing to employees in this respect. Raises given for all kinds of other reasons are indistinguishable to the employee from raises given for improved performance. In many cases a periodic increment in salary is given almost automatically provided the employee's performance has not slipped in any marked and obvious way since the last raise. This is not a matter of cost of living; *other* adjustments are made to compensate for that factor. Often a raise will be given *in the hope* that it will motivate the individual to higher performance. Sometimes it is given to prevent his becoming dissatisfied. Sometimes the message is: "No raise next time *unless. . . ."*

It is almost universally true that management stresses as a major responsibility of every manager the "development" of his subordinates. Yet raises *and promotions* are regularly given to managers who are notoriously incompetent in this respect or who ignore this responsibility in an attempt to obtain higher productivity or lower costs.

During a study of management development practice in some twenty-five blue-chip companies a few years ago, I queried representatives of middle and lower management concerning the extent to which they perceived salary increases to be related to successful effort in developing subordinates. By far the most common response was a cynical smile! In only two or three companies did there seem to be a genuine perception that the relationships between these factors amounted to more than "talk."

Performance with respect to managerial control systems (such as budgeting, scheduling, and quality control) should, one would suppose, be associated with extrinsic rewards as well as punishments. My observation, however, leads me to the conclusion that the relationship is seldom perceived this way by middle- and lower-level managers. They *do* perceive a *long-term statistical probability* of extrinsic rewards for better than average performance along these lines, but there is a very high and relatively immediate certainty of *punishment* for mistakes, failures, and sub-standard performance. As we noted in Chapter 8, the motivational significance of control systems generally appears to be escape from punishment, not the pursuit of extrinsic rewards.

The power available to management through the control of extrinsic rewards and punishments is used primarily in the same fashion as legitimate authority: to gain compliance. Even though its potential for producing positive contributions to organizational goals is limited, this potential is not by any means fully realized in practice because the rewards are not consistently and equitably linked with performance.

Approval and disapproval represent another way of exercising power through control of extrinsic rewards and punishments. Recognition is a widely used form of approval. The problem of equity enters here also.

Likert reports a situation in which a group of women employees *who had reached the top of their salary bracket and who could not be promoted to a higher job* were praised by their superiors for their outstanding performance.[5] Their reaction was openly expressed dissatisfaction. If they were doing such a fine job, why were they not promoted, or at least given salary increases?

Perhaps the most significant thing about approval and disapproval is that they are a form of power exercised effectively by *peers* as well as by superiors. Social man generally desires membership in his work group. In fact, one of the more powerful punishments is exclusion from the group. British workers use the device of putting a man "in Coventry" as an extreme punishment. His fellow workers behave as though he doesn't exist. Few individuals are strong enough to endure this punishment for long.

The approval of peers is often stronger than that of the manager

[5] *Likert has discussed this finding at various management conferences. In a personal communication to us (Apr. 19, 1966) he writes: "We have encountered this situation also in other forms and one of these I have published [New Patterns of Management. New York: McGraw-Hill Book Company, 1961, chap. 7]. It deals with personnel in a large utility who were over forty years of age and who had high school education or less. They were seeing young people with college education promoted around them. Consequently, every time their superior praised them for a job well done, it reminded them of the discrimination they were experiencing. They were not being promoted. Younger, less experienced and from their point of view, less competent people were being promoted around them to superior positions." (Eds.)*

when behavior approved by the latter is disapproved by the former. One of the prime forces behind restriction of output, and the other behavior associated with it, is the power of group approval or disapproval. It is stronger than the combined power of financial incentive and managerial approval.

This form of power, then, is useful to the manager, but only under certain conditions. He must be selective in its use, depending upon other relationships between E and I variables. If work-group goals and his own can be successfully linked, the group can become a powerful asset.

IDENTIFICATION

Another form of power rests on identification. When an individual genuinely identifies himself with a group, a leader, or a cause, he is in effect saying that the goals and values associated with that cause have become his own. He then self-consciously directs his efforts toward those goals and gains intrinsic satisfaction through their achievement. In fact, if the identification is strong enough, the individual will forgo many extrinsic rewards; he will risk censure, disapproval, and other punishments in the service of the cause.

Identification is the basis of the "power of example." One must recognize that the setting of examples has virtually no value unless there is identification. It is not uncommon for a manager to say of a superior to whom he reported in the past: "He certainly taught me how *not* to behave." The term is awkward, but this might be called "negative identification."

It is in connection with identification that *leadership* becomes a source of power. The general outcomes of behavioral science research challenge the conception that leadership is a "property" of the individual. It is no more a property of a person than gravitation is a property of physical objects. Leadership, like all other phenomena we have been examining, is a *functional relationship* between E variables (*including* the personal characteristics of the leader, who is a part of the environment of his followers) and I variables (including the needs, goals, expectations, and values of the followers). Identification with the leader—because it represents an attractive means for achieving desired goals—is a necessary condition of the relationship.

Depending upon *other* characteristics of the system (both *I* and *E* variables), certain personal characteristics of the leader may be especially relevant. However, these are not identical among all successful leaders. In fact, the search for the *unique common characteristics* of the successful leader has proved fruitless.

The youth and vitality of John F. Kennedy made him an attractive symbol to many Americans. On the other hand, Eisenhower was attractive as a leader because of quite different personal characteristics. Some people identified with one, some with the other, and some with both.

The central point is that when there is identification, not only is the legitimate authority of the leader enhanced, but there are intrinsic satisfactions associated with that identification. Commitment to common goals is a characteristic of the relationship. Self-direction and self-control in the service of those goals are natural outcomes of that commitment.

People identify not only with leaders, but with important groups ("reference groups," the sociologists call them), with organizations (from which category industrial organizations are not excluded), and with causes. The accomplishments of American industry during the two major wars of this century were in large measure a function of identification with the national cause, and therefore with the subsystems associated with that cause.

It is often asked how the commitment characteristic of a crisis can be created under normal conditions. The answer, I believe, is the one I have repeated so often that it becomes trite: By creating conditions such that organizational members can achieve their own goals *best* by directing their efforts to the achievement of organizational goals. This is the basis for identification, whether with a leader, a group, a cause, or an organization.

The paradox—worth pondering—is that when there is high identification, with its concomitant commitment to goals, the exercise of authority and other forms of external reinforcing influences becomes at the same time more effective and less necessary. What Mary Parker Follett called the "law of the situation" is one illustration of this paradox. When there is identification with organizational goals, the members tend to perceive what the situation requires and to do it whether the boss exerts influence to have it done or not. In fact, he need not be present or even aware of the immediate circumstances.

Identification is a variable. Its intensity appears to be related both to the *importance* (to the individual) of the goals that he believes may be achieved by the identification and to the *number* of such goals.

The strong identification with organizational goals that develops among employees of successful Scanlon Plan companies is related, I believe, to the range of needs involved.[6] The bonus is an extrinsic reward associated primarily with physical and security needs. The social structure by which ideas for improvement are generated and evaluated offers rewards associated with social needs and provides for membership, approval, status, and recognition. The participation in problem solving offers a variety of intrinsic rewards, including a greater than normal degree of autonomy (control over one's own actions) and opportunities for achievement.

A final point: The perception of *movement toward* relevant goals is important for maintaining identification, not their absolute accomplishment. In fact, *full* accomplishment would remove the basis for the identification. At the other extreme, the perception of no movement toward the goals ultimately brings disillusionment and reduces identification to zero.

The creation of conditions (relationships between E and I variables) that yield identification is a potent source of power. Its value is often underestimated. The reason, I believe, is that "power" so often means "getting people to do what I tell them to do." While identification does tend to increase the legitimate authority of the manager, a much more significant and valuable consequence is that people will direct *their own* efforts toward the goals that are the basis of the identification and will exercise *self-control* in achieving them. This does not represent power to some managers *unless the identification is with them personally*.

Let us say that a manager succeeds in helping a group of subordinates organize their work in such a fashion that performance of the group task becomes an exciting and challenging effort. It offers them significant opportunities to use their combined talents and ingenuity, to achieve greater control over their own fate, to develop new knowledge and new skills, to gain satisfaction from their membership in a cohesive team. Once such a situation is created, effective performance of the task becomes to a considerable degree a result of these motivations rather than of the manager's direction and control. In fact, if he attempts too

[6] F. G. Lesieur, *The Scanlon Plan.* Cambridge, Mass., and New York: Technology Press of M.I.T. and John Wiley & Sons, Inc., 1958.

much direction and control, he may decrease these motivations and lower the workers' performance. They have become identified with the group task, and the "power" lies in that identification. The manager's role shifts in some respects to that of a helper, a remover of restraints, a teacher.

It is unlikely that a manager with a mechanical conception of motivation, or a manager with strong personal needs to control others, would even attempt to create a subsystem with these characteristics. It represents the very antithesis of what he means by exercising power. Yet such a unit may make fully as effective a contribution to the goals of the larger organization as one which has developed a strong *personal* identification with its manager and has thus enabled him to exercise substantial power directly.

It is obvious that individuals can become identified with leaders or groups or causes whose goals are opposed to those of the industrial organization. The tendency of many managers is to attribute this kind of negative identification either to outside organizations like unions or to troublemakers or agitators inside the organization. Although these assumptions may be true, negative identification can and does occur as a fairly direct consequence of managerial policies and practices. Let us consider an illustration.

A company has established an individual incentive plan in its production units. In one unit, each individual's job has been studied by an industrial engineer who, in addition to timing the job and setting an incentive rate for it, has carried out motion studies and shown each worker how to perform his particular task in the most efficient way.

Over the course of time, these workers have developed certain attitudes toward the incentive program. They are suspicious of the industrial engineer. They believe that if their incentive earnings get too high, some excuse will be made to change their jobs and retime them. They fear that they will end up doing more work for less pay. They perceive many inequities in the plan: unsatisfactory allowances, loose rates on some jobs, tight ones on others. They perceive management to be controlling them closely and limiting their opportunities to control their own actions. They perceive the inspector to be arbitrary in his rejections, thus obliging them to do unnecessary work at day rates.

One worker in the group—articulate, somewhat more aggressive than the rest, highly skillful in deceiving the engineers who time the jobs— symbolizes the common frustration and antagonisms of the group. Under his informal leadership they become a cohesive team. The task with which they are now identified is a protective one, aggravated by their hostilities. It is to beat the system. It is, however, an exciting and challenging task involving real risks that enhance the challenge.

Many of the rewards obtained by the group described earlier are now obtained by this group. They can exercise their talents and their ingenuity; they have some feeling of greater control over their own fate; they can develop new skills; they are members of a cohesive team that provides opportunities for gaining approval and status by certain kinds of contributions to the goals with which they are all identified.

As for the manager of the group, they may like him as a person, but they cannot identify with him because he symbolizes the values and goals of the system they are dedicated to defeat. He has power stemming from his position. If he is not too demanding, they will let him exercise it. However, unless he sides with them against the engineers and the inspector and the unreasonable aspects of the plan (an unlikely possibility), he is a part of the system with which they are negatively identified. Identification with that system or with him would be traitorous.

An extreme example? Distorted? Not at all. It has been repeatedly experienced and documented for decades. Moreover, such situations are not necessarily caused by unions. They are found in unionized and nonunionized plants alike.[7]

Such an outcome is not, of course, a *necessary* consequence of the installation of an incentive plan. It *is* the consequence, however, of certain relationships between E variables and I variables in which the former are largely under management's control. It *is* the consequence of ignorance or disregard of the transactional character of all forms of managerial influence. It *is* the consequence of a mechanical conception of motivation that places exclusive emphasis on extrinsic rewards. It *is* the consequence of exercising authority without regard to perceptions of legitimacy and equity. It *may* also be the consequence of the belief that leadership (in the case cited above, by the first-line manager) can be effective independent of other characteristics of E and I.

PERSUASIVE COMMUNICATION

The last of the several methods of exercising power that we shall consider is persuasive communication. Communication can serve

[7] *Rensis Likert has suggested the following reference to us as supporting evidence: S. B. Mathewson,* Restriction of Output among Unorganized Workers. *New York: The Viking Press, Inc., 1931. (Eds.)*

several purposes. It may be a means of giving information, of expressing ideas or feelings, or of influencing others. Our concern here is with the last of the three.

Communication used persuasively is an "input" to a system (individual, group, organization, etc.). It is the most frequently used input. All *social* interaction—as opposed to inputs from the physical environment—involves communication. The basic point to be kept in mind is that the system to which communication is addressed is not passive. The message as received is always "processed." It may be accepted, modified in any of a variety of ways, or rejected in part or in whole. Even the apparent failure to receive it may involve unconscious processes. *What is done to the incoming message depends on the characteristics of I and E.*

Communication intended to affect one part of the system (the intellectual characteristics of I, for example, such as knowledge) may be significantly altered by other parts (attitudes and feelings) or by characteristics of E (organization structure of existing policies) and thus influence the output. Thus a mere comment about a situation or event, intended to have no influence on behavior, may sometimes result in a major response. Top executives are often surprised that a purely casual remark made during a visit to the field may lead to the expenditure of a substantial amount of energy because it was interpreted as a request for action. The obverse may also be true: A major attempt to influence behavior by communication may have very minor effects.

We know a moderate amount about how the characteristics of the system affect the response to communication. From experiments we find that when subjects are asked to describe the characteristics of an individual on the basis of observing his photograph, their replies will vary widely and quite predictably depending on whether they were told that he is a union leader or a business executive—that is, on their perception of his role. The influence of an individual introduced into a group that is carrying on a discussion or attempting to make a decision will be small or great depending on whether he is perceived to be of higher or lower status in the organization hierarchy than the group members.

There is a tendency among managers to ignore such "system characteristics" and to assume that the effects of communication depend almost entirely on the characteristics of the communication.

Thus organizational difficulties of all kinds are attributed to "poor communication," and time and money are expended in improving the inputs.

There is a lot of evidence to show that variations in the nature of the input do have differential consequences. The fields of advertising and public opinion polling provide detailed, systematic knowledge of such relationships. However, the significance of these is relatively small compared with the significance of the relationships between the communicator and the characteristics of the system. For example, if there is mistrust on the part of the audience toward the communicator, differences in the form and style of his communication will have very little effect on the response. If, on the other hand, the relationship is one of high mutual trust, large variations in the skills of the communicator or the form of the communication will not materially reduce their effectiveness.

It is a fairly safe generalization that difficulties in communication within an organization are more often than not mere symptoms of underlying difficulties in relationship between the parties involved. When communication is ineffective, one needs to look first at the nature of these relationships rather than at ways of improving communication.

A related aspect of what is often a rather naïve faith in the power of communication as a method of persuasion is closely connected with management views of "rational-emotional" man: "Tell them the reasons and they will do what we want." Management tends to assume—quite naturally but often incorrectly—that its decisions and policies are rational and objective. It further assumes that "proper communication" will transform its audience into rational recipients. Thus the primary requirement for obtaining compliance with management's desires becomes that of making sure that the reasons for a given action are understood. Of course, this is a necessary requirement, but it is by no means sufficient. Considerably more important are the characteristics of the system to which the communication input is made.

The head of a large manufacturing unit in one company has strong feelings about the moral obligations of his employees to work hard. He expresses these by saying that they should be willing to give nine hours of work for eight hours' pay. He does not feel that these expectations are in any way emotional. They are coldly rational, and he can expand

on the reasons at length. His own personality is paternalistic, but in a
rather cold, patriarchal way.

For years he has dominated his organization—his management as well
as the workers. But recently there have been increasing signs of resistance. Despite the generous benefits that he bestows on his employees,
they have become restive under his close control. The union leaders,
themselves strongly antiauthoritarian, have used the situation to exploit
mistrust of him and what they term his "exploitative" methods. Grievances are frequent and bitterly fought; legalistic technicalities dominate
negotiations. For example, several pages in the union agreement are
devoted to rules about the assignment of overtime. A series of strikes
has occurred, and the situation is becoming steadily more explosive.

This manager is firmly convinced that the solution to this whole
complex of problems lies in "effective communication," particularly
between first-line supervision and workers. Moreover, effective communication will be achieved, he believes, if he can somehow get these
supervisors to "take an interest in their subordinates." They must find
out about each worker's family, his hobbies, his day-to-day problems at
home. Then it will be possible for the supervisors to explain management's position, including the necessity for high productivity and high
quality. When the workers are thus "informed," the problem will resolve
itself. They will no longer listen to "the lies and the misinformation
being peddled by the union."

This situation is extreme, but it is also classic. In my experience
it is repeated constantly at varying levels of intensity, entirely outside the field of union-management relations as well as within it.
The underlying set of assumptions are ubiquitous: management's
reasons for its policies and actions are rational; subordinates
would react rationally and accept them if they were properly informed; better communications would inform them and solve whatever difficulties exist. The same assumptions underlie the attempts
of staff groups such as operations research teams, accountants,
engineers, and even many personnel managers to persuade line
managements to accept and utilize their proposals, their improved
methods, their programs.

Human beings demonstrate over and over that they don't respond
in the desired fashion to tactics based on these assumptions. The
reaction then tends to be either that people are "ornery" by nature
or that the communication was ineffective. The problems involved
are often aggravated by the common admonition: "You have to
sell them."

There is a fascinating question about all this. Management almost universally today agrees readily to the proposition that two-way communication is essential. Why, then, is there such heavy reliance on one-way communication? I have become convinced that a major reason is in the conception that many managers have of two-way communication. They believe that it consists primarily in discovering the questions or objectives generated by a management communication *and answering them.* Two-way communication is not conceived to be a transaction at all, but a means of ensuring that others understand what is being communicated. Since what is being communicated is obviously right, rational, and reasonable—if they understand, they will be persuaded.

As a behavioral scientist, my conception of two-way communication is that it is a process of *mutual* influence. If the communicator begins with the conviction that his position is right and must prevail, the process is not transactional but coercive. The process is one-way no matter how many words may be said by those receiving the communication. Even if it takes place in a face-to-face situation, it is as much one-way as mass-media advertising.

In a discussion of clinical counseling, Carl Rogers made a profoundly insightful observation that in my view applies far more widely. He said: "I can only be helpful [as a therapist] to another person if I can permit myself to understand him."[8] He then pointed out the significance of his use of the word "permit." It is that if one undertakes genuinely to *understand* another, one runs a risk of being changed oneself in the process! This, I have come to believe, is a major reason why genuine two-way communication is a rare phenomenon indeed.

There is massive evidence from behavioral science research that communication aimed at changing others (without the genuine possibility of even a small reverse influence) is effective only to a very slight degree. Bauer, in the paper referred to earlier, cites some examples. Speaking of commercial advertising, he says:

> Consistently successful commercial promotions convert only a very small percentage of people to action. No one cigarette now commands more than 14 per cent of the cigarette market, but an increase of one per cent is worth $60,000,000 in sales. This means influencing possibly 0.5 of all adults and 1.0% of cigarette smokers. This also

[8] *For a fuller view of Rogers' work, see Carl Rogers,* On Becoming a Person. *Boston: Houghton Mifflin Company, 1961. (Eds.)*

means that a successful commercial campaign can alienate many more than it wins, and still be highly profitable.[9]

He also refers to some calculations he has made on the famous Kate Smith war-bond campaign which elicited $39 million in pledges. Somewhere between 2 and 4 percent of her audience were influenced to make pledges.

Studies of political campaigns show quite conclusively that their influence is largely limited to the "undecided" portion of the population (although those already siding with one party may have their convictions reinforced by that party's campaign efforts).

The results of such one-way communication may be of great practical value to advertisers and politicians, but they are very small in terms of the proportion of a population influenced. This is the sobering thought that management might keep in mind when it seeks influence within the organization by means of persuasive communications. The qualification to this admonition is that persuasive communications can be highly effective when they are appropriately related to the characteristics of the system. One way of achieving such relationships is to rely on transactional communications, but the risk is that the communicator himself may be influenced in the process.

SUMMARY

We have examined legitimate authority, control of extrinsic rewards and punishments, identification, and persuasive communication, which are four methods for exercising power (influence) in organizational settings. Each has value; each has limitations. The appropriateness of each (i.e., the degree to which it is likely to achieve desired ends without negative side effects) is a function of the characteristics of the system to which it is applied. No one form of power is inherently or generally more effective than any other. All are necessary causes of human behavior; none is a sufficient cause.

The effectiveness of every form of power is limited—or *enhanced*, depending on one's point of view—by the fact that all social influence is transactional in nature. There is virtually no such thing as

[9] R. A. Bauer, "The Obstinate Audience: The Influence Process from the Point of View of Social Communication," *American Psychologist*, vol. 19, no. 5, p. 322, May, 1964.

unilateral influence because the human being (as well as the group or organization) is an open, organic system. Every input to this system is modified or transformed. Outputs of a human system can therefore be successfully predicted and influenced only if inputs are appropriately related to the characteristics of the system being influenced. Often, if not always, consideration must also be given to the larger system of which the subsystem being influenced is a part.

Social influence—the exercise of power—is thus a far more difficult and complex process than is typically understood by such labels as hard, soft, or firm-but-fair strategies of management. However, the selective exercise of power based on knowledge of the system involved offers the possibility of considerably more effective organized human effort. This is the contribution of the behavioral sciences to one important aspect of the managerial task.

part five

**TEAMWORK
AND TENSION**

10

building a managerial team

THE NATURE OF A MANAGERIAL TEAM

There are significant differences between a collection of individual managers comprising an organizational unit and a managerial team, even though the team label is usually applied indiscriminately to both. The organization chart does not distinguish between them. Both may be described broadly in terms of the formula $B = f(I,E)$, but the significant differences lie in the specific characteristics of I and E, and particularly in the relationships between individual group members. (At the risk of repetition, I should reiterate the general meaning of this formula. Basically, it is a notation for the idea that behavior cannot be understood unless all the forces operating on a certain unit of behavior are understood. The two main forces are those relating to the individual, such as his personality characteristics—I variables—and those relating to the environmental forces—E variables.)

Some of the differences are like those described by the Tavistock group in contrasting conventional and composite forms of organization in the coal mines (see Chapter 6). In the conventional form, you will recall, the members of the unit were responsible for the performance of discrete, specialized tasks defined by industrial engineers and assigned by the manager. Control of the unit's performance was maintained by the manager through rewards and punishments applied to individuals separately. The structure was static. The interaction within the unit was largely between the manager and individual members in two-person relationships. The relations between members tended to be competitive because the system structure and controls produced such behavior.

The *typical* managerial unit—the top management of a major subsystem like a plant or a division or a large accounting department, or of the company as a whole—possesses the same characteristics. The specialized individual tasks are larger and more complex, and they are defined by the organization chart and position descriptions rather than by industrial engineering principles. Individuals are assigned to the defined positions by the head of the unit. The controls are more elaborate, but in the end they are applied by the head of the unit to his subordinates individually. The structure is static. The primary, meaningful interactions take place between the manager and the individual members separately, even though there may be some lateral interaction between subordinates as well as some group meetings. Their relations are basically competitive as a natural consequence of the form of organization and the controls.

What is here called a managerial "team," on the other hand, is an altogether different system that more closely resembles the composite organization in the coal-mine study. There are unique features in this kind of managerial system, which we shall examine in a moment; but first let us look at the gross similarities. The chief characteristics of a composite system are these:

1. The unit as a whole has one *primary task.*
2. Its *flexible structure* adjusts to the demands of the situation.
3. Controls are *transactional.* All members of the unit, including the manager, determine the structure, the responsibilities, and the subgoals of the unit; the principles and the norms governing its operation; and the standards of performance.
4. Opportunities for *intrinsic rewards* associated with membership in and accomplishments of a cohesive group are deliberately created, while control of *extrinsic rewards* is maintained by management. Extrinsic individual rewards, particularly salary, are determined by administrative procedures that emphasize *equity.*
5. All these characteristics are operational within limits defined by the larger organizational system.
6. *Cooperative relationships* exist between the members accomplishing the common primary task.
7. *Interdependence* between all the members (the "subsystems") determines the survival and successful performance of the team.
8. Members must have appropriate skills.

The characteristics of any sociotechnical system are in part determined by the technology around which the social organization is formed. The "technology" of a managerial team differs in obvious ways from that of a work team organized around machines and physical-chemical processes. The activities are largely of an intellectual, communicative, problem-solving nature (including the emotional components). They require the use of power in influencing human behavior rather than the manipulation of physical objects.

As a result the relationships between team members and the operational procedures are necessarily different. Let us then consider some of the unique features of an effective managerial team.

AN EFFECTIVE MANAGERIAL TEAM

1. Understanding, mutual agreement, and identification with respect to the primary task.   This is a matter of determining "what business we are in," and it requires far more examination and discussion than when the primary task is production of a component or a product or maintenance of physical equipment by a work group.

2. Open communications.   Sound decisions, *and their successful implementation,* whether related to the internal operation of the team or the performance of its primary task, must take into account *all* the relevant facts. As indicated earlier, feelings and emotions are relevant facts. They are inextricably interwoven with intellectual facts and logical arguments in rational-emotional man. Moreover, depending on the relationships within the team, intellectual ideas, objective facts, and logical arguments relevant to the problem or issue under discussion must be publicly available to be utilized by the group. If members do not put them on the table—for whatever reasons—the group cannot take them into account. Genuinely open expression of ideas *and* feelings—what some have referred to as "leveling"—is a necessary condition for effective functioning in a managerial team.

Although group members (and some group managers) often say with real conviction that communications within the team are completely open, experience indicates that such a condition is rare indeed. One of the important T-Group learnings for many participants is the discovery of the tremendous gap between what passes for open communications in everyday organizational life and what is potentially achievable.

One qualification is necessary at this point—one that applies widely. *Virtually every variable associated with human interaction may be "dysfunctional" at both extremes.*[1] Like other variables, the

---

[1] *This particular point grew out of long and frequent discussions that Doug held with Jay Forrester on the application of industrial dynamics to the human side. (Eds.)*

openness of communications is relative for all practical purposes, not absolute. Even in the most intimate personal relationships—marriage, for example—*absolutely* open communications could destroy the relationship. At the other extreme, completely closed, phony communications would have the same result. The relativity, then, is to considerations of the effect on the "other" and on the relationship, and we shall consider that in a moment.

The general point here is that there is a wide range between the extremes in which the more open the communications, the better for team functioning, *given certain other characteristics of the system.* The absence of these other characteristics is one of the major causes of relatively closed communications in many managerial teams. One of these is the desire, discussed earlier, to keep emotions out of the situation—to achieve complete rationality and objectivity. This is impossible, although magical rituals make it possible to pretend otherwise.

3. Mutual trust. Unless mutual trust is a characteristic of the system, the openness of communications (as well as the effectiveness of other aspects of team operation) will be severely limited. The meaning of "trust" is simple to taste, but it is a condition difficult to achieve—particularly under conventional forms of organization. Trust means: "I know that you will not—deliberately or accidentally, consciously or unconsciously—take unfair advantage of me." It means: "I can put my situation at the moment, my status and self-esteem in this group, our relationship, my job, my career, even my life, in your hands with complete confidence."

Again, the variable is dysfunctional at the extremes; again, most managerial groups operate in a range well below the appropriate level; again, the form of organization (particularly the stress on individual competition) affects the degree of trust that is practical.

Trust is a delicate property of human relationships. It is influenced far more by actions than by words. It takes a long time to build, but it can be destroyed very quickly. Even a single action—perhaps misunderstood—can have powerful negative effects. It is the *perception* of the other person and of his actions, not the objective reality, on which trust is based. And such perceptions are profoundly influenced by emotions: needs, anxieties, guilts, expectations, hopes.

Thus, mutual trust and open communications are closely interrelated. Open communications help prevent misperceptions of actions, but inconsistencies between words and action decrease trust. Openness clearly involves genuineness and honesty. Argyris speaks of "authentic" communications, and this may be a better term than "open" for conveying the complexity of the meaning.[2]

The effective performance of a managerial team is in a basic and fundamental sense a function of open communications and mutual trust between all the members, including the leader.

4. Mutual support.   Support is a variable ranging from a negative extreme through zero to a positive extreme. The negative range is characterized by an attitude of hostility; zero is indifference; the positive range is an attitude reflected in behavior like caring, concern, help, friendliness, love.

Support can take on characteristics of sentimentality or of "help" that encourages dependency, but that is decidedly not what the term is intended to mean in this context. It is, rather, a predictable absence of either hostility or indifference between members of the team (including the leader) that enables each member to be more himself, to feel less necessity for fighting to obtain his "rights" or for defensive or protective actions. He is freed to contribute more fully his "assets" to the primary task of the unit.

5. Management of human differences.   This involves one of the paradoxical aspects of organized human effort. Human differences represent both a major asset and a major liability in team action. Differences—not only in training, experience, and capability, but in all the emotional aspects of man discussed earlier—are the stuff of progress and improvement in social life. All innovations, all creative problem solutions, all successful new social or political or economic developments rest ultimately on the fact of human differences. If it were not for these, environmental changes would result typically in passive adjustment rather than active coping.

On the other hand, human differences are a liability in *organized* human effort. Certain kinds of differences, unless controlled, can readily destroy the organization. Unless some norms and rules and

[2] C. Argyris, *Interpersonal Competence and Organizational Effectiveness.* Homewood, Ill.: Irwin-Dorsey, 1962.

procedures are fairly uniformly followed, anarchy rather than organization results.

However, if the control of differences is too tight—whether it is exercised by the manager on the group or by the members on each other—the asset represented by the differences will be buried under an array of pressures for conformity and the members will become a collection of organization men.

More specifically, the very existence of individual differences creates a potential for disagreement and conflict over almost any issue or problem that may arise in the course of the team's performance of its task. The management of conflict, rather than its suppression, is essential in order to reach decisions or solutions that will be implemented successfully rather than sabotaged. Management of differences, rather than either suppression or abdication in the face of conflict and disagreement, is also essential to creative decisions rather than mediocre, least-common-denominator compromises.

Failure in the management of individual differences is the source of many negative attitudes toward group operation. It leads to the conviction that groups cannot make decisions, that the pressures of group conformity destroy creativity, and that groups are by nature inefficient and time-wasting.

We shall examine in some detail in the next and final chapter the strategies available for managing human differences. For the moment it is sufficient to note that their successful management is an essential characteristic of an effective managerial team.

6. Selective use of the team.   Not all managerial activity is appropriately carried on in a group setting. Use of the team for team activities and appropriate delegation to individuals or subgroups of other activities are characteristic of effective overall team performance.

The choices involved are not always simple or appropriately determined by procedural rules. This variable, like the others, is conditioned by a number of factors. For example, if mutual trust is low, an important feature of internal group control will be a low degree of delegation and the necessity, therefore, for many group meetings. Certain group tasks require frequent interaction between members; others do not. The interdependence of the subtasks that together comprise the primary task may be high or low; it may vary through time predictably or unpredictably.

7. Appropriate member skills.   The combined skills of the members of a sociotechnical system must be such as to meet the technological requirements of the primary task. The skills required of the membership of a managerial team are therefore quite different from those of a work team performing, for example, a mining task. Among the activities common to managerial teams, some are concerned with the performance of the task while others—*equally necessary*—are concerned with the "maintenance" of the team as a viable system. Table 3 lists a number of activities that have been found to be characteristic of overall team operation. Obviously certain skills (and attitudes, too) are required for effective performance of these activities.

TABLE 3*

Task Roles	Maintenance Roles
Initiating activity	Encouraging
Seeking information	Gatekeeping
Seeking opinion	Standard setting
Giving information	Following
Giving opinion	Expressing group feeling
Elaborating	Testing for consensus and commitment
Coordinating	Mediating
Summarizing	Relieving tension
Testing feasibility	
Evaluating	

* *These roles or functions represent a composite and representative list drawn from a variety of sources and summarized by Bennis and Shepard. [Warren G. Bennis and Herbert A. Shepard, "Group Observation," in W. G. Bennis, Kenneth D. Benne, and Robert Chin (eds.), The Planning of Change. New York: Holt, Rinehart and Winston, Inc., 1961, pp. 743–756.] (Eds.)*

A common belief is that these functions or activities are the responsibility of the team leader. This list constitutes the definition of a major part of his role. Logically, however, the necessary and *sufficient* requirement is that these roles be performed effectively. My own experience in T Groups and consulting work confirms the logical implication: Team effectiveness is correlated with the performance of these activities, not with their performance by any particular individual.

In fact, I have at times observed a negative correlation between team effectiveness and the degree to which the leader takes sole responsibility for all these activities. Part of the reason for this is that their skillful performance by one individual alone represents an impossible task. Even if he possessed all the required skills, the complexity and the pace of group operation is such that no single human being could perceive everything that goes on well enough to know when one of these activities rather than another is needed.

The second reason for the negative correlation is more important: If the members of the group sit back and leave the performance of all these activities to the leader, it can mean that they are not identified with either the group or the task. If they are identified, if they are committed to the task, they will quite naturally—given the opportunity—become involved. Involvement means relevant activity, and relevant activity consists in the performance of these functions as the situation requires.

No one member need become the specialist in any one of these functions, although individual differences tend to produce varying degrees of specialization. Roles like the "conscience of the group," the "devil's advocate," the "navigator," the "oilcan," the "tension breaker" are familiar in everyday experience. The specialization in most teams is considerably less narrow than this. Any member may at any time perceive the necessity for a given function to be performed—perhaps when the other members are too intent, or too emotionally involved, to recognize the need—and either perform it himself or alert the group to the necessity.

8. Leadership.   We have looked briefly at seven characteristics (all of them *variables*) that affect the performance of a managerial team. There are others, but these are of major significance. They are interdependent: each of them is influenced by the others. They are not *unique* to the managerial team in contrast to other sociotechnical systems, but they are perhaps more prominent and more important in affecting the performance of the primary task of such a team.

One other major characteristic of all forms of group effort remains unexamined until now, although I have mentioned it in several connections. Most managers would probably consider it *the* determining characteristic. That characteristic is the leadership— the personal qualifications, skills, role, and strategy—of the manager of the team.

I do not wish to undervalue leadership. However, in the face-to-face group (as opposed in some respects to the large system like the company or the total society) the nature and role of leadership may be perceived very differently by the manager and many behavioral scientists. In explaining group behavior, many managers would find this formula quite adequate:

$$B_{\text{group}} = f(L_{a,b,c}\ldots)$$

where $L_{a,b,c}\ldots$ represents the characteristics of the leader. *It is this perception (implicit or explicit) that is a major causal factor behind the majority of existing company programs for the selection, training, and development of managerial personnel.* It is this perception that lies behind managerial preoccupation with the discovery of "potential for advancement" among employees. In turn, this perception is intimately related to the perception of humanity as being divided three ways: into the hopelessly inadequate, the average men, and the few.

Some findings that are emerging from behavioral science research suggest,[3] on the contrary, that the explanation of group behavior—of organized human effort at the subsystem level anywhere in the managerial hierarchy—requires a formula like this:

$$B_{\text{group}} = f(M_{a,b,c}\ldots T_{f,g,h}\ldots O_{l,m,n}\ldots L_{q,r,s}\ldots E_{u,w,x})$$

where M includes the attitudes, knowledge, skills, and capabilities of the members; T includes the characteristics of the primary task of the group; O includes the structure and internal controls of the subsystem; L includes the skills, capabilities, and other characteristics of the leader; and E includes a large number of variables in the larger organizational system and in society.

The behavior of the group is importantly influenced not only by the nature and degree of each of these many variables, but by an array of relationships between them. The characteristics and behavior of the leader are not *the* determining variables; they are necessary but by no means sufficient. The nature of the variables and of the relationships between them makes the characteristics of the leader crucial or relatively unimportant as a determinant of group performance.

Some of the *necessary* characteristics of the effective team (in

[3] *For an excellent review of the research literature, see* A. Paul Hare, Handbook of Small Group Research. *New York: Free Press of Glencoe, 1962, chap. 11.* (Eds.)

any function, and at any level of the organization) *cannot be determined by the leader alone,* no matter how skillful or capable or competent he may be. Open communications, mutual trust, and natural support may be helped or hampered, or even eliminated, by the actions of the leader, but he cannot bring about a high degree of any of them by the exercise of any of the forms of power available to him. They are characteristics of the system, affected by many other variables in the formula, and their degree is determined primarily by attitudes and interaction of *all* the individuals in the group, including the leader.

It is important to note finally that variables like leadership, open communications, mutual trust, and mutual support are among the characteristics of a group as a system that differentiates it from the mere sum of the individual subsystems which *in their interaction* create the group. The significance of these variables for group performance could not be predicted on the basis of knowledge of the characteristics of individuals. Study of the group as a group reveals their existence, their nature, and their importance.

Perhaps it is now clear why an effective managerial team seldom just happens. It is a complex and delicate system, the building and maintenance of which requires much time and attention. Its contribution to the achievement of the goals of the enterprise can, however, be well worth the effort devoted to its creation.

TEAM DEVELOPMENT

The skills involved in social interaction are often compared to those involved in sports like golf and tennis. Since the concern here is with team skills, the analogy to baseball or football teams might appear to be appropriate. However, these analogies are too oversimplified for our purposes. The common aspect is the necessity for practice, for experience-based learning. One cannot acquire the skills of golf without playing golf, nor can one acquire the skills of team operation without being a team member. Beyond this, however, the analogy between the two forms of activity tends to become misleading, perhaps dangerously so.

There is little in a sport that requires intellectual knowledge or more than primitive theory. One can become an expert golfer without acquiring or using scientific knowledge. One may not acquire great proficiency by simply buying golf clubs and balls and going out to play golf, but little harm is likely to ensue.

With respect to professional skills such as those of the doctor or lawyer, real harm may result from sheer trial-and-error learning. This is why society does not permit the would-be doctor to practice his profession until he has acquired a body of intellectual knowledge and certain skills under the supervision and guidance of experienced professional practitioners and scientists. To the extent that management is becoming a profession, similar considerations apply.

Relatively little attention has been given until fairly recently to the mental and physical consequences of subjecting industrial employees at every organization level to managerial strategies developed largely by sheer trial and error, guided only by the goal of profit maximization. Both medical and behavioral science research have begun to provide evidence that these consequences are by no means trivial. Executive "casualties"—fatal and nonfatal—attributable to the strains created by the organizational environment are now known to be considerably more frequent than in the population at large. A little-known fact of great significance is that the casualties among lower levels of supervision are *more* frequent than among top executives.[4] Studies of mental health in industry conducted by the Institute for Social Research at the University of Michigan are providing evidence that managerial strategies affect much more than the economic success of the enterprise.[5]

I have introduced this apparent diversion because concern has been expressed during the past few years that methods of training in team development (particularly those called "sensitivity training," which involve the use of T Groups) are potentially dangerous. It is alleged that they introduce strains that can have deleterious effects on the psychological adjustment of participants in such a program.

Such possibilities do exist, but it seems to me important that we keep them in proper perspective. The possibilities of permanent harm to human beings from these methods of training—provided they are conducted by people who have *appropriate professional competence*—is considerably less than that inherent in the conditions of everyday life in most industrial organizations.

Two cautions are in order. The first is that management would be wise to assure itself of the professional competence of people

[4] S. V. Kasl and J. R. P. French, Jr., "The Effects of Occupational Status on Physical and Mental Health," in J. R. P. French, Jr., R. L. Kahn, and F. C. Mann (eds.), *Journal of Social Issues,* vol. 18, no. 3, pp. 67–89, July, 1962.
[5] French, Kahn, and Mann, *op. cit.*

offering formal training in team development. Second, do-it-yourself approaches to managerial team development should be undertaken carefully and with awareness of the dangers involved. This is not to say, however, that the self-development of managerial teams involves greater danger along these lines than is inherent in many widely accepted managerial policies and practices with respect to such mundane things as budgeting, cost control, promotion, and performance appraisal.

Let us say that a manager wishes to undertake a process of team development involving himself and all his immediate subordinates, both staff and line. In my view this is perfectly appropriate and practical. He is concerned with changing certain characteristics of this sociotechnical system. He cannot impose these conditions on the group, as we have seen. Nothing can be gained by any kind of secret manipulation of the system. The process must be public and transactional. He would begin, therefore, with an open discussion in a meeting of the whole group. He would discuss his reasons for suggesting such a process. If he were tentative, perhaps even doubtful (which would be natural), he would say so. He would encourage a discussion about its feasibility. He would ask his subordinates to express their own feelings openly, because there would be little point in the process in the face of strong reservations. If negative reactions were expressed, however tentatively, he would be careful not to override them or even try to persuade. Instead he would encourage the group to understand them fully.

He would need to be prepared with some ideas (not firm convictions) to answer questions like: "How would we go about it?" One way would be to discuss the primary task of the group with the purpose of clarifying and coming to mutual agreement about it.

If this process is to be transactional, it will involve much more than a cursory examination of the organization chart and the position description of the members' jobs. It will involve a critical, deep analysis by the whole team of the role pressures to which they are subjected and of the implications of these for what the organization expects of this unit formally and informally.

From this analysis will follow an attempt to formulate the primary task that encompasses all these expectations. If, as often happens, this proves impossible, the discussion will proceed to determine what *is* possible, from the point of view of both the team and the larger organization.

The outcome may be a conception of the team's primary task that resembles neither the formal organization chart and position descriptions nor the role expectations of the organization as experienced by the team. If the analysis conducted by the group and the manager has been thorough, they will have a persuasive rationale for seeking change in one direction or the other. The manager would normally be the person to attempt this.

If the group's conception of its primary task is acceptable, there remains the organization of work within the team. Members should be given considerable freedom in working this out themselves. The ideal would be a structure of responsibilities that is flexible enough to permit adjustment to changing situational requirements whether these arise within the team or in the wider organizational system or in the external environment of society (which of course includes the market).

The overall value of a process like this is not only the classification that results, but the growth of identification with the team and its responsibilities, and the sense of a degree of control by the group over its environment. There will have been compromises and adjustments, but the active involvement of the whole team and the sense of achievement when the task is completed provide important intrinsic rewards to all the members.

A second step—or possibly an alternative first step—would be to analyze together the current state of the group, to attempt to agree on those characteristics which require improvement.

I have seen groups make effective use of a simple rating scale like the accompanying exhibit for purposes of analysis. After a little discussion of the meaning of each of the variables, each member fills out the form anonymously, rating his personal view of the current state of the group. The ratings are then pooled and a chart prepared by a couple of members showing the mean of the ratings and the high and low "score" for each variable. On the basis of these data, the group discusses what aspects of its group operation need work.

Analyzing team effectiveness.[6]   Analyze your team (the group here in this room) by rating it on a scale from 1 to 7 (7 being what you consider to be ideal) with respect to each of these variables.

[6] *This form was developed by McGregor in conjunction with John Paul Jones's group at Union Carbide Corp. for their own team development. (Eds.)*

Then (with the rest of the team) discuss in depth the situation with respect to each variable, paying particular attention to those for which the average rating is below 5 or for which the range of individual ratings is particularly wide. Formulate some ideas about *why* these perceptions exist. The "whys" are likely to be quite different for different variables.

---

1. Degree of mutual trust:
   High suspicion _____ High trust
   (1) (7)

---

2. Degree of mutual support:
   Every man for himself _____ Genuine concern
   for each other
   (1) (7)

---

3. Communications:
   Guarded, cautious _____ Open, authentic
   (1) (7)

   We don't listen to   We listen; we under-
   each other ───────────────── stand and are understood
   (1) (7)

---

4. Team objectives
   not understood by team _____ Clearly understood
   by team
   (1) (7)

   Team is negative   Team is committed
   toward objectives _____ to objectives
   (1) (7)

---

5. Handling conflicts within team:
   We deny, avoid, or   We accept conflicts and
   suppress conflicts _____ "work them through"
   (1) (7)

---

6. Utilization of member resources:
   Our abilities, knowledge,   Our abilities, knowledge,
   and experience aren't   and experience are fully
   utilized by the team _____ utilized by the team
   (1) (7)

7. Control methods:		
Control is imposed on us _____	We control ourselves	
(1)	(7)	

8. Organizational Environment:		
restrictive; pressure	Free; supportive;	
toward conformity _____	respect for individual	
	differences	
(1)	(7)	

In using an approach like this, it is important to agree in advance on a ground rule that there will be no attempt to ferret out the "author" of any individual rating, although any member may *volunteer* comment about his own rating. If the group leader feels comfortable about it, his ratings might also be used. However, in most circumstances it would be advisable to wait until a fairly high degree of mutual trust and open communications is revealed by the data before attempting to analyze the leader's behavior separately.

The ratings of most groups tend to be unrealistically high on the first attempt to use an instrument like this. After some initial discussion it is usually fruitful to wait a week or two and then use it again, applying it the second time to a regular group meeting concerned with normal operating problems. A few minutes before .the close of the meeting can be set aside for the purpose.

There is no reason, of course, why a group cannot devise its own instrument, using variables that are felt by the group to be most relevant for diagnostic purposes. Trends can be obtained by repetitive use of the instrument to help the group keep track of progress. In my experience it is unwise, however, to devote a lot of time and energy to building elaborate and precise instruments. The tendency then is to become preoccupied with the mechanics rather than the data. The purpose in using such devices is not precise measurement, but the provision of information that provokes analytic discussion.

The problems that provide the agenda for meetings of the team, whatever they may be, are grist for the mill with respect to group development. The way to use them for this purpose is first to provide time for looking back directly after the group has dealt with a problem in order to examine together "how we operated." The experience is fresh; the data for examination are the behavior of the group members (including the leader) as they carried on the normal activities of the group. The process involves comments by individual members, if they feel free to express themselves, on how they felt when this or that happened and on their reaction to the whole process.

The group will gain most from such a feedback process if they give consideration to the consequences of different kinds of feedback. One of the purposes is to help each member of the group to recognize the impact of his behavior on others. Under ordinary circumstances individuals rarely acquire this information, *particularly* with respect to an immediate and specific situation when all the details are "here and now." More often than not, an individual discovers that the reactions of others to his own words or actions are not the same as he perceived them to be. Thus the feedback provides him an opportunity to test his perceptions against reality and to modify his future behavior *if he chooses to do so.*

If this is a purpose of feedback, it is quite unlikely to be helpful if it takes the form of a critical attack that simply puts the person on the defensive and makes it unlikely that he will either understand or accept the feedback. Nor is there any help in feedback that attempts to probe the motives behind his behavior. To turn feedback into a "two-bit analysis" defeats the purpose and may be highly disturbing to the recipient.

The guiding notion is that feedback tells the other individual: "This is how your behavior affected me." The information should be authentic. If his behavior made me angry or suspicious, or if it led me to become his ally or to feel especially positive about him, or if it led me to agree or disagree with him—*I should try to help him to understand my reactions, my feelings.* If others provide him with feedback on the same basis, he may discover that my reactions were like those of others in the group or that they were quite different. (In the latter case *I* may learn something, too!) The same considerations would apply to feedback by an individual member to the rest of the group.

Honest, sincere feedback between all the members of a team (including the leader) is one of the foundations on which mutual trust is built. It is in this sense that open communications and trust are reciprocal. It may seem inconsistent to think that one can be supportive and at the same time tell another person: "Your behavior angers me." However, there is a tremendous difference between responding with anger (attacking) and feeding back information about one's feelings in the hope of correcting a situation that is interfering with group accomplishment. The same is true of a reaction of mistrust or indifference or rejection. Genuine feedback of this kind (information) *identifies a problem that can be explored* and probably solved.

I argued earlier that *absolute* open communication may be dysfunctional. In the context of the immediate situation one must always make judgments about how far to go. The problem in the ordinary situation is that feedback (if it occurs at all) is so limited and cautious that it seldom provides much help. My experience with groups that are deliberately trying to create mutual trust, support, and open communications is that most people are quite skillful in sensing intuitively when they are at the limit in a given situation. Subtle cues from the other person—gestures, flushing, particular verbal responses, and the like—are noted. In a group setting particularly, it is remarkable how often some member will respond to these cues, even if the individual giving the feedback does not, and will find ways to divert the discussion. This is fortunate because there are no simple rules for setting the limits. Human beings differ widely in the amount and kind of feedback they can accept. On the other hand, the limits are not fixed. They usually become extended substantially as mutual trust and support increase.

Of course, these skills and sensitivities are not immediately present when a group begins to use this method. Discussion of the reasons for using feedback and examination of what the reactions are as the process goes along can pretty well prevent any lasting damaging consequences.

The process of using feedback to explore and examine a just-ended group session can gradually be extended so that many difficulties arising in group operation are corrected as a matter of course almost as they happen rather than being postponed to a post mortem. Part of the skill acquired is in recognizing when it is important to interrupt an ongoing activity in order to save time and trouble later and when to refrain from doing so because it is recognized that the effects on group performance are relatively unimportant. During the initial phases of acquiring skill along these lines, groups often become unduly preoccupied and overly sensitive about the needs for feedback on minor matters. This is, however, a natural and useful part of the process of acquiring skill.

Intellectual, cognitive learning is also an integral part of effective team development. This can occur in two different ways, and both are important. I have stressed continuously throughout this volume the many ways in which beliefs, assumptions, perceptions of reality, and theories about the nature of man and organized human effort affect managerial strategy.

Thus, effective use of feedback *for purposes of team development* requires another step: generalization. The value for the group in undertaking an analysis of their behavior is not in the analysis itself, but in what can be learned from it that can be used to improve the future performance of this and any other groups with which these members may be associated. For purposes of group development it is not enough that a particular problem may have been solved. The particular problem may never appear again in exactly the same form. However, it may well appear again under other circumstances and in other guises. Will the analysis of this single experience help the group to recognize the problem in other forms and deal with it? The probability is "no," unless the group has answered for itself the question: What have we learned from this experience? The learning may pertain to the meeting that was analyzed or the process that was used for analysis, or both. The generalizations may be quite tentative, subject to modification as a result of future experience. Nevertheless, the group's conscious generalizations concerning its own learning are the rungs of the ladder it is seeking to climb.

Every time the group faces a business problem that cannot be solved easily and quickly on the basis of habit, past experience, or existing policy, there is an opportunity for team development. Blake and Mouton refer to this as the "dilemma-invention-feedback-generalization" process, and it is in many ways a model for all kinds of learning.[7] A dilemma or problem confronts the group (or the individual). If it is solved by conventional, known formulas, there is no learning. If, however, it can be solved only by some form of ingenuity or inventiveness (or if that ingenuity is used to find a new and better solution to an old problem), there is an opportunity for learning by analyzing how the solution was arrived at and generalizing on the analysis.

That is why feedback, whether simple, brief, and essentially intellectual (as it will be sometimes) or complex, time-consuming,

[7] R. R. Blake, *Tenth Proceedings of the Action Research Training Laboratory*, West Point, New York, 1960.

and emotion-laden, is crucial for team development. This is what is implied by "experience-based" learning.

Generalizations and theories developed by others—particularly if systematically based on research—can also be used by a team to aid its own development. In this field of human behavior (unlike more abstract disciplines), it is generally found that the practical usefulness of theory depends to a considerable degree on the closeness of its relation to experience.

Immediately after arrival at M.I.T. a group of Sloan Fellows spent five days in a training program designed to help them enter a new situation and become active, effective members of a new organization (M.I.T.) rapidly and without the disturbing and debilitating worries that so often encumber this process (whether in education or in industry). The program design involved them actively in analyzing what they needed to know and in providing administrative, faculty, and student "resources" to help them find the answers.

On the morning of the fourth day, a member of the staff gave a lecture that included a number of research-based generalizations with respect to the psychological difficulties typically encountered by human beings in entering and becoming effective members of new organizations. The lecture dealt with emotional phenomena like unconscious anxiety.

The staff felt that the content would have been rejected as theoretical or impractical *if it had been presented on the first day.* After the experiences these men had had during the three previous days, however, they gave the lecturer their rapt attention and asked a number of highly insightful and penetrating questions when he had finished. Just before the lecture session adjourned, the staff member asked the group what they felt they would have learned from this lecture if it had been presented on the first day as a theoretical guide and rationale for the program (which in fact it was). The audience hooted with laughter!

A managerial team, then, engaged in self-development, can accelerate learnings if they can read and discuss appropriate books and articles, or listen to and discuss lectures by outside experts, *particularly* when the content is associated with their own current developmental experiences. Although this is not easy to do, it is by no means impossible.

Consultation—even by correspondence with a behavioral scientist active in this field—is a relatively simple way to obtain suggestions for reading, provided only that the group can tell him what they are currently attempting *to do* in their self-development program. A staff team discussed earlier has encouraged its members to go to one of the formal programs in this field. As a result they now have several members who have gained familiarity with the literature of the field and who can therefore suggest appropriate reading as the team needs it. Another method is to use the help of a consultant who sits with the team periodically to aid them in their self-development efforts. Such a person can provide direct inputs of theory at appropriate times, as well as suggest relevant books or articles.

When such direct guidance is unavailable, the references in a book such as this can perhaps be explored by a member of the team in search of relevant material. The librarian in a university can often be helpful in such exploration.

The basic point is that some knowledge of existing theory can guide a group engaged in self-development, not alone by the discussion it provokes but by providing generalizations to be tested by the group both in selecting the strategies it uses for carrying out its primary tasks and in attempting to improve group maintenance.

Clearly, I believe that a managerial group sincerely interested in its own development along these general lines *can* successfully undertake its own self-development, with or without the help of a behavioral scientist consultant. There are advantages and disadvantages in the do-it-yourself approach, but they are there in other approaches as well. My experience leads me to conclude that the only answer to the question of which is best is: "It depends on circumstances." This may appear to be ducking the issue, but I have learned that I cannot offer even a tentative answer until I know quite a bit about those circumstances. One needs at least a rough knowledge about many I and E variables in the particular situation in order to form a judgment. A group that undertakes such an analysis of its own circumstances can usually decide what approach to take, at least for a trial period.

An alternative approach to team development is to make use of formal training. There are many ways of doing this. Some organizations today have staff trainers who are professionally competent to undertake in-company work along these lines. Sometimes internal staff members can arrange to bring in trainers for the purpose.

A more common approach is for one or more members of the team to go to a formal program such as those conducted by the National Training Laboratories or its affiliates as a preliminary to undertaking team self-development. There the individual can obtain some genuine personal learning (if he is open to it), familiarity with the underlying theory of team operation, some awareness of methods of learning that have been well tested, and access to the literature.[8]

It is sometimes difficult or impossible for a whole team to attend such a program for a week or even two weeks, but this does happen, and NTL, for example, is prepared to include such teams as units in a larger program. The advantages of this are considerable. The whole team undergoes a series of common experiences that can set it well on the road to further development upon returning home. Even when the whole team cannot go simultaneously, there are advantages in having at least two members go together.

I share with most of my colleagues the conviction that formal training of this kind under the guidance of a competent professional staff is a valuable experience *for the manager who goes because he wishes to go.* It is questionable whether the same value accrues to the man who goes because someone else thinks he needs it. Such a man is apt to be so preoccupied with why he was sent that he is simply not in condition to learn much. If he was sent because he has real problems in this field, in the hope that he will be "cured," the prognosis is dismal. The man himself gains little or nothing; he may be severely threatened. In addition, his fellow participants are often prevented from learning what they could learn because of the effects of his presence on the group.

This training is not a cure for anything. It is designed to help normal, competent managers (who are already effective in their relationships with other members of their organizations) gain greater insight and understanding with respect to the complexities of organized human effort and acquire some of the knowledge that the behavioral sciences can contribute to this field. Moreover, the lasting value of their learning from this training will depend heavily on the degree to which members of the "system" to which they return (and other aspects of the environment) permit and encourage the learning to continue. The man who has gotten all there is from such a program is launched on a long-term educational venture; he is not "educated" in the complex field of organized human effort by a week or two of training.

There are today some major efforts in team development involving all the members of large organizational units (such as a refinery or

[8] E. H. Schein and W. G. Bennis, *Personal and Organizational Change through Group Methods.* New York: John Wiley & Sons, Inc., 1965.

a bank). Blake and Mouton describe a series of steps extending over several years that carry such a unit through the process of organizational development along lines consistent with the theory discussed in this volume.[9] An assessment has recently been published of one such effort.[10] Much more work and research is needed before we can understand all the relevant I and E variables.

SUMMARY

Conventional organizational theory has focused almost exclusively on the individual as the main building block of the organization and has tended to ignore the problems of groups or teams and their development. Changes that have affected organizational life over the past twenty-five years have forced students and practitioners alike to reexamine these trends. Certainly, a strong strain of individualism is alive in all of us nurtured in the spirit of democracy. However, the complexity of the environment and the goal structure of the enterprise create a situation in which it is no longer possible to comprehend or conduct the operation of the enterprise without some form of teamwork and team building.

Team development is infinitely more complicated than personal development. We still know little about it, although some findings in small-group research and clinical practice, as well as direct experience in evolving T Groups, have added to our knowledge. More understanding is needed concerning the nature of certain variables, both I and E, as well as their complex relationships.

What we can say about team development is this: (1) As in other processes of development, time and historical continuity are important. There is no reason to expect that a new committee or task force will function efficiently at its inception. (2) Groups and teams, like other organisms, require internal communication and leadership functions and, in addition to time, the development of a common language and culture. (3) Teams have to interact and cope successfully with an environment and, like other open systems, to

[9] R. R. Blake and J. S. Mouton, *The Managerial Grid.* Houston, Tex.: Gulf Publishing Company, 1964.
[10] R. R. Blake, J. S. Mouton, L. B. Barnes, and L. E. Greiner, "Breakthrough in Organizational Development," *Harvard Business Review,* November-December, 1964.

process and store large amounts of information necessary for survival. (4) Finally, teams have to succeed in mastering their tasks and achieving competence.

Without a clear recognition of the importance of teams, what blocks and facilitates their development, and under what conditions they are appropriate, management may not be fully utilizing their potential human resources.

11

the management of differences

Most human beings are ambivalent about conflict. On the one hand we revel in it; successful competition is the source of highly significant rewards, both extrinsic and intrinsic. Every form of sport, for example, involves conflict that we enjoy. Some people find the greatest pleasure in directly participating in sports; others enjoy primarily the spectator's role. Many find pleasure in both roles.

If we are participants in a sport, there are the extrinsic rewards of social approval and status associated with winning or being a member of a winning team. In professional sports there is money in addition. For many of us the intrinsic reward inherent in the act of winning is the most powerful. Even as spectators, we identify with individuals or teams, and we are elated when they win, depressed when they lose.

Even *personal* conflict has its positive aspects; we often obtain intrinsic rewards from creating an artificial competitive situation within ourselves and then struggling to win by beating the standard that we have established. Golf contains this element of personal conflict even when we play with others.

Conflict in organization life is associated with extrinsic and intrinsic rewards in many ways. Successful competition by the firm in the market place is, of course, a major example. So is competition within the organization through the processes of promotion. Problem solving—overcoming obstacles of all kinds—is a form of competition in which the win-lose conflict may be completely impersonal (a machine breakdown, a performance standard or sales quota, an engineering problem), or it may be quite personal, such as beating some other group's performance or finding a better solution to a problem than some one else has found.

Virtually every successful innovation—technical *or* social—is the outcome of conflict between the new and the old. Even the broadest kinds of social progress can be perceived in this light. Competition and conflict are pervasive in all social interaction. One important reason lies in the very nature of man. Winning, overcoming obstacles, solving problems are the source of fundamentally important rewards. The evolutionary roots of this phenomenon are obvious.

On the other hand, many if not all human beings deplore, even hate, certain forms of conflict. A strike can be the source of intense frustration to management, and the conflict leading up to it often appears wasteful and unnecessary. Conflicts between individuals or departments, between managers at different organizational levels, or between staff and line groups may interfere seriously with the total organization's accomplishment. Broad conflicts within a society or between societies are often tremendously costly not only in economic terms but in terms of human welfare and human life. Juvenile delinquency and divorce, as well as many mental and physical illnesses, are the symptoms of conflict.

Thus some forms of conflict and competition are perceived to be good and desirable, whereas others are perceived to be destructive, undesirable, and morally or ethically bad. It is clear that when we argue about the relative merits of competition and cooperation, or about the desirability of eliminating conflict, we ought to consider the kind of conflict that we have in mind.

The issue is not a simple one; some forms of conflict are both desirable and undesirable. This phenomenon is characteristic of relationships within managerial teams. Such teams consist of individuals who differ from each other not only in experience, knowledge, and capabilities, but in emotional characteristics of all kinds (attitudes, values, beliefs, styles, perception of reality). On the one hand these differences provide the essential ingredients of innovation, creative problem solutions, organizational achievement. On the other hand these same differences are the source of *inevitable* conflict and disagreement that may interfere with effective group and organizational accomplishment. They can lead to major inefficiency, delay, and frustration and to least-common-denominator decisions and highly unsatisfactory compromises.

Thus the competitive, win-lose type of conflict[1] which is an asset and a source of individual reward is simultaneously a liability and a source of frustration within the organizational setting of the management team. Under these circumstances ambivalence with respect to conflict reflects a genuine reality-based paradox. Individual differences are *both* an asset of great value and a major liability.

The dilemma thus created is found in every form of organized human behavior, although it is particularly visible in the face-to-face group. Organized forms of human activity can be successful only if there is a high degree of cooperation among individuals and

[1] *This is sometimes more technically referred to in game theory as a* zero-sum *game and is defined as a transaction in which one party can win only at the other's expense.* (Eds.)

integration of individual effort. At the same time, such cooperation and integration *inevitably* reduce individual freedom, lessening the possibility that individuals can contribute fully in terms of their personal characteristics.

Virtually all attempts to deal with this inherent dilemma of organizational life have entailed restrictions of individuality and individual freedom. The chaos and disorder of anarchy are too inconsistent with man's needs for order and predictability to be seriously contemplated. Historically the practical issues have always centered around the degree and nature of such limitations. In fact, we are dealing again with a psychological variable that is dysfunctional at *both* extremes. *Complete* conformity is as impractical—in fact, as unthinkable—as complete individual freedom. Neither has ever been found in social organizations. Human ingenuity will make *all* forms of social interaction transactional even under the most coercive controls that man has ever devised. At the other extreme, complete anarchy would virtually eliminate social interaction. The evolutionary developments discussed in Chapter 1 would suggest that anarchy in this complete form could occur only in biological species *below* the mammal.

STRATEGIES OF MANAGING DIFFERENCES

Let us first examine some ways of dealing with this dilemma in the face-to-face group. Obviously the characteristics of the system are different at different levels. But certain aspects of conflict are similar within the individual, in the two-person relationship, in the face-to-face group, and in larger systems such as the total organization, the nation, and between nations. Since the face-to-face group is a major focus of attention throughout this volume, it seems appropriate to use the small group as an exemplar of the processes of managing differences.

Observation of the processes of decision making and problem solving in management leads to a rough categorization of three different strategies in dealing with interpersonal conflict: (1) the strategy of divide and rule, (2) the suppression of differences, and (3) the working through of differences. Of course, there are many tactical differences within each one. However, there are broad distinctions between the three with respect to the use of power and the system variables that are controlled. Also there are distinguishable differences in outcomes.

DIVIDE AND RULE

The divide-and-rule strategy is an attempt to maintain control of differences by confining them to a series of two-person situations in which the superior can utilize the power of his position in the organizational hierarchy. The tactics associated with this strategy are really methods for preventing conflict and disagreement from *arising in the group situation.* If group meetings are held, they are primarily for the purpose of giving and getting information or formalizing decisions that have in fact already been made. The superior may discuss problems or issues with subordinates in order to utilize their knowledge, skill, and experience, but he is careful to promote interaction between individual subordinates and himself and to discourage interaction between the subordinates themselves.

This strategy clearly prevents the development of a managerial team. It stimulates competition (for the boss's favor) rather than cooperation between the subordinates. Rivalry, hostility, secrecy, and minimal lateral communications are characteristic. If the superior is himself talented, innovative, and politically adept, he can make the strategy workable. However, he will tend neither to select nor to develop strong, talented subordinates. Problems of succession are likely to be severe in his organization. Above all, the asset represented by human differences will be unrealized because he perceives such differences as a liability: a threat to power.

Finally, commitment to decisions affecting the whole group is likely to be minimal with such a strategy. Each subordinate becomes dedicated to building and protecting his own empire. There is little of the give and take that can lead to genuine acceptance of decisions for the good of the whole organization. Consequently, the superior must devote a substantial amount of time and energy to exercising close surveillance over his subordinates to ensure that his decisions are implemented. Elaborate control systems are a necessity under the strategy of divide and rule.

This strategy tends to be attractive to the manager who is preoccupied with a personal need for power and who holds an essentially pessimistic view with respect to the motivation and competence of his subordinates. (Note the circular aspect: Because he needs power, he will tend to select weak rather than strong subordinates who, in turn, will demonstrate the correctness of his pessimistic view.) In short, the strategy of divide and rule is consistent with a Theory X cosmology.

Environmental causes may sometimes make this strategy a short-run necessity for dealing with human differences. Within certain political environments it would be foolhardy to utilize any other approach. It is often used, however, in situations where it is inappropriate.

SUPPRESSION OF DIFFERENCES

A second and widely accepted method of dealing with differences within the managerial team is to suppress them. The tactics used for this purpose are many. One is to ignore them, to pretend that they are irrelevant. Another is to demand objectivity and rationality —often expressed in phrases like "Let's be objective," "Let's stick to the facts." (These magical tactics were discussed earlier as devices for eliminating the effects of emotion on decision.) Another tactic, a favorite of the courtly chairman of a board of trustees on which I once served, is: "Let's not be divisive, gentlemen. We all have the best interests of this organization at heart."

A fourth tactic involves a kind of arbitration natural to the hierarchical organization: The leader decides in favor of one alternative after hearing the arguments for each. A fifth is to decide the issue by a majority vote. The vote is an appropriate and necessary device at another system level: when a large population is deciding an issue. It is rarely appropriate in a face-to-face situation.

All these tactics are tacitly assumed to eliminate conflict, to settle disagreements, to make it possible for the group to proceed with its business. In fact, as we have seen earlier, the tactics work only when the issue is of little consequence to anyone. When the differences between people in the group are real, when feelings are involved, these tactics create a situation in which it is no longer legitimate to argue, or discuss, or express disagreement openly. Differences are suppressed; they are not eliminated. In fact, it is precisely these devices for dealing with differences that constitute the pressures for conformity so often deplored in group action.

The behavioral consequences of the suppression of differences are readily observable in managerial teams where this strategy is predominant. The effects on the implementation of decisions are particularly evident. These range, depending on a number of other factors, from a passive ("letter but not spirit of the law") compliance, through subtle forms of conscious and unconscious sabotage, to outright rebellion. Lip service is often given to the idea that a subordinate who is overruled after being given an opportunity to "speak his piece" will then be a good soldier and enthusiastically carry out whatever decision is reached. This idea is largely a myth even when the subordinate's conscious intent is to do so. Human emotions are not so easily disregarded.

Another consequence of reliance on the strategy of suppression is that the asset represented by these differences cannot be realized. In the desire to get action, to be efficient, to save time, to keep emotional factors from interfering with rational action, the possible creative uses of conflict are forgotten. The perceived liabilities of human differences loom too large.

One other consequence of the strategy by suppression is often observable: protective behavior of many kinds. This is less obvious and less formalized in managerial teams than in larger systems. Robert's Rules of Order represent a system of elaborately formalized protective devices within a strategy that relies primarily on suppression of conflict (by vote). The ingenious uses to which these and similar protective procedures can be put are well demonstrated in political organizations such as the United States Senate.

When tactics other than voting are used to suppress conflict, as is typically the case in managerial teams, the protective devices tend to be less formal but they are usually present. They include such things as lining up support in advance of a meeting, getting decisions from the leader on important issues without even bringing them up for group discussion, preparing and presenting proposals (including factual data) in ways that disguise underlying issues, wrangling over trivial or irrelevant details in the wording of a policy or decision, involving staff groups in "busywork" to protect a position or to undermine that of an opponent. The list of such tactics is inexhaustible; the effects on the efficiency of team performance are obvious. They are natural consequences of a strategy of suppression of human differences. They are not inherent characteristics of groups.

WORKING THROUGH DIFFERENCES

The third strategy involves the working through of interpersonal or intergroup conflict, rather than its denial or suppression, and it is usually a planned strategy. It cannot be successful except in a committed and reasonably mature managerial team. It can lead to different and less damaging consequences. This strategy does not always or even frequently produce unanimous decisions. Important differences—intellectual and emotional—are expressed, openly examined, and laboriously explored. Sometimes the process fails and it is necessary to revert to a decision by the leader or to the vote. More often it results in the kind of understanding that can lead to changed beliefs and attitudes and can resolve the conflict; or it may bring about a consensus in which there is genuine commitment to a given decision even though differences remain. Sometimes it leads to a truly innovative outcome.

The strategy of working through offers several significant advantages. First, the interplay between members (including the leader) in their search for a resolution of their differences is precisely the process that most often yields innovations. To be sure, it is an individual who produces a creative idea initially, but that process can be stimulated and enriched by human interaction in an appropriate climate. The strategies of divide and rule and of suppression create a climate conducive to conformity and compromise and to winning an argument rather than discovering the best answer. These are inimical to creativity. It is reliance on these strategies for dealing with human differences which leads many people to conclude quite erroneously that only the individual (presumably in isolation) can be creative.

Second, when the working-through process is successful, all the members are genuinely committed to the implementation of the decision reached. Management often seriously underestimates the costs in time, energy, and money of ensuring that a decision is carried out when the commitment to it is low or absent. Such costs are substantial. In fact, many important decisions are virtually nullified because of the difficulty in getting them properly implemented. Even when an individual conscientiously decides to be a good soldier after his views have been overruled or denied expression, his performance will, for unconscious reasons, be considerably less than optimal. Consider how often we as individuals fail to carry out decisions that we ourselves have made, but to which we have little commitment.

Third, the strategy of working through builds and strengthens relationships within the group while the other two strategies tend to undermine them. The functional interdependence between the members of a management team demands a high degree of cooperative effort. As noted above, when the strategy for dealing with differences is divide and rule or suppression, a win-lose orientation inevitably develops, and the result is often a kind of competition between members in which it is more important to support or protect a position than to reach the decision that is in the best interests of the organization. Mutual antagonisms, secrecy, playing politics, currying favor with the leader—all tend to develop within the group. Only a consistent strategy of working through differences can minimize these detrimental consequences.

REQUIREMENTS FOR WORKING THROUGH DIFFERENCES

The process of managing conflict by working through differences— in contrast to denying or suppressing them—is complex and difficult. There is no simple technique like the use of authority or the vote for accomplishing it. The leader alone cannot manage conflict, but he and the group together can do it. They must start by creating certain underlying conditions, modifying certain *group* variables which, as we have seen, are hard to change but, once established, can be maintained.

The first of these necessary conditions is *authentic communications* among the members and between them and the group leader. This means that each member (including the leader) is genuinely free to express his real feelings, as well as his intellectual ideas, openly in the group. It means also that such expressions will be sympathetically explored by the group until they are fully understood (although not necessarily agreed with). It means that other members (or the leader) will not intentionally ride roughshod over any individual's views or his feelings, or express snap judgments publicly or privately about his competence or his value to the group because his expressions may seem deviant, unclear, or even irrational. It means that every member of the group (including the leader) will understand what is involved in genuine listening and will have acquired some skill in this difficult art.

Managers often assert and sometimes really believe that communications are authentic and open within the groups they lead. In fact, however, this condition seldom exists under the pressures typical of hierarchical organizations. The norm of "objectivity," the negative attitude toward emotion, and the power relationships within the group typically create a situation in which open communication would be foolhardy. Concentrated effort of a skilled kind, extending over months or even years, is necessary to bring about a high degree of authenticity in communications within a managerial team.

Obviously, authentic communications cannot be produced by fiat, by an order, or even by a plea from the leader. They depend on certain other related conditions. Among the most important of these is a climate of *mutual trust and support* within the group (see Chapter 10). In such a climate, members can be themselves without fearing the consequences. They perceive that even within the competitive struggle for power and status and the other rewards of corporate life, their fellow members and the leader will not take unfair advantage of their openness—and their attendant vulnerability.

In such a climate one does not find an absence of strenuous argument. However, people are not playing ping pong on top of the table while rolling bowling balls at each other underneath it. Conflict and disagreement have a different quality (and vitally different consequences) when the group climate is one of mutual trust and support rather than of indifference or suspicion or hostility. In the latter case, important contributions to the decision are often lost in the struggle to gain a competitive advantage or to protect oneself from attack.

There are a number of other variables involved in the successful working through of intragroup conflict, but I shall mention only one: *genuine respect for differences* among the members, whether these be in ideas, knowledge, attitudes, emotional adjustment, or special competence. Again, lip service is often given to this condition, but the real, unexpressed attitudes are seldom consistent with it. In private conversation outside the group many such differences are negatively evaluated, weaknesses rather than strengths are emphasized, deviant behavior is criticized, individuals are perceived as currying favor with the boss or as passing the buck to avoid criticism. It is a difficult thing to achieve genuine respect for another human being, particularly if he does not share one's own values or if he does not possess the particular characteristic one most admires in others.

When respect does exist, on the part of the leader toward the members as well as between members, each individual can achieve and maintain his own identity and pressures for conformity are minimal. It becomes recognized by all that genuinely creative solutions to problems can best occur under such conditions. Human differences and the conflict arising from them are seen not as threats to effective group performance, but as the means for the achievement of high performance.

The primary point, then, is that authentic communications, attitudes of mutual trust and support, and genuine respect for individual differences are requirements for managing conflict and disagreement in the interests of effective group decision making. Although these are individual actions and attitudes, *they have no meaning except in terms of interaction with others.* They are variables appropriate to the group as a system. Moreover, they are primarily emotional variables although they have intellectual content also. None of these crucial group variables are considered when the strategy of decision making is to divide and rule or to suppress conflict.

An additional point of some significance is that the leader cannot, by his own efforts alone, create these conditions. He can facilitate their development by removing obstacles to open communications, or he can hamper their growth if, for example, he fosters excessive competition between his subordinates or is unable to be open in his relationships with them.

Conditions in the wider social, political, and economic environment of the group are also important. These are in part modifiable by the leader, depending upon his level in the organization and the upward influence he wields. For example, organization structures and accounting control practices that foster narrow departmental loyalties, empire building, or staff-line conflict can prevent the development of the group conditions necessary for successful team decision making.

When managers are unaware of these relationships between group variables, when they attempt to control group behavior by manipulating individual variables exclusively, when they believe group performance to be a function of leadership alone, when they perceive human differences to be phenomena that interfere with effective decision making, it is perhaps small wonder that managerial teams appear to be liabilities rather than assets.

THE PROBLEM OF TIME FOR TEAM DEVELOPMENT

Some would argue that the time required for the development of these relationships and for managing conflict along these lines makes the whole idea preposterous, that a group operating this way would never be an efficient decision-making device. Management, they feel, cannot take months or years to develop the necessary attitudes and skills. Work has to be performed!

The issue is one of comparative advantage. A group that makes good decisions, innovates successfully, and carries out decisions effectively and enthusiastically is worth a great deal. If, in addition, the development of these group characteristics is accompanied by better problem solving, better planning, higher motivation, and greater commitment to organizational goals, the comparative advantage is considerable.

In practice the time "wasted" in following a working-through strategy of decision making is far less than one might suppose. When there is mutual trust and support, many issues are recognized to be unimportant which under other conditions would be the subject of great concern. Defensive and protective behavior diminishes. Only the truly important differences—those which involve deep feelings or significant conflicts of ideas—require working through. Along with the development of conditions like those discussed above come a change in the members' and the leader's ideas of what is worth fighting about and a willingness to stick to relevant issues rather than to devote time and energy to establishing superiority over other members, defending the ego, or building checks and balances into the decision for protective purposes.

In addition, when mutual trust is high, there is a genuine willingness to delegate many decisions from the leader to individual members and by members to each other. "Whatever you decide will be all right with me," becomes one expression of the mutual trust and respect existing in the group.

Finally, the members of a genuinely effective team in which the climate is healthy do not need to be together in a face-to-face relationship in order to function effectively. Like a healthy family, the members act as team members whether they are geographically in proximity or not. In fact, another of the assets of an effective managerial team is that, because there is a higher level of mutual trust and support, fewer meetings rather than more are required. It is in such a context that genuinely autonomous *individual* action becomes possible. This is the reason for my earlier assertion that there is no necessity for choosing between the individual and the group.

Management is generally willing to spend substantial amounts of time and money in training and developing individual managers. Because of the attitudes and cultural values mentioned above, and because of lack of awareness of the importance to the organization of *group* competence, relatively few firms are yet willing to invest time and money on group development. Yet programs of group development contribute substantially to individual development, whereas the reverse is not true. *The team setting, provided the group variables discussed above are at optimal levels, is the ideal environment for individual learning and growth.* We recognize this with respect to the family, but the implications for the managerial team are seldom appreciated.

EDITOR'S POSTSCRIPT

Ironically, this chapter was the least finished draft of all eleven chapters that constituted the original manuscript. It is the one to which Doug was most committed and what he left is a partial foundation for others to complete and build upon.

One thing that future students of conflict in management and other areas might consider is Doug McGregor's own life-style. For it is clear that he exemplified what his writings were moving toward, namely, a great capacity for managing differences between diverse groups. As Beckhard has said in his Introduction, Doug enjoyed "multiple memberships" in groups that not only do not talk to each other but are often not on speaking terms. Doug somehow brought them together. In effect, his entire life, professionally and personally, was a "bringing together," a creative "working through" toward a new consensus. Men like Doug McGregor, if understood, may throw new light on the management of differences.

One last word. Doug was a cautious optimist, meaning that hope just shaded reality. He felt that the management of differences and the development of effective problem-solving teams (the focus of Chapter 10) could never be fully realized. But he urged us on to work for and hold high these commitments where no easier alternatives can be seen or respected.

INDEX

INDEX